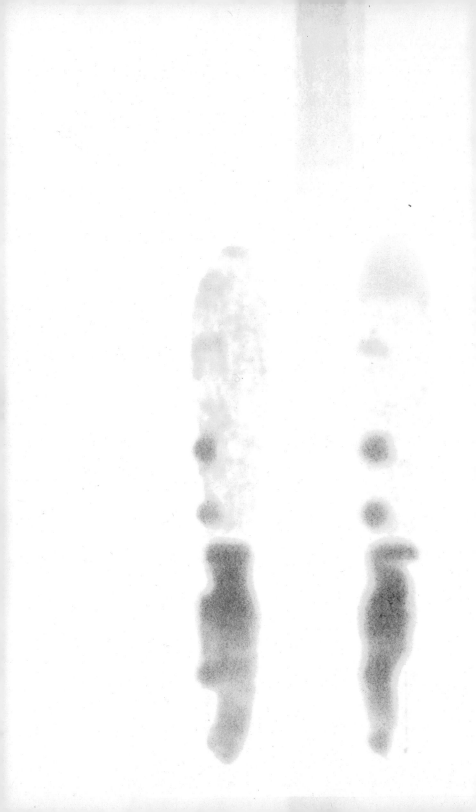

THE NOVELS OF MARGARET DRABBLE

DISCARD

THE NOVELS OF MARGARET DRABBLE:
Equivocal Figures

Ellen Cronan Rose

Barnes & Noble Books
Totowa, New Jersey

First published 1980 by
THE MACMILLAN PRESS LTD
London and Basingstoke
Companies and representatives
throughout the world

First published 1980 in the USA by
BARNES & NOBLE BOOKS
81 Adams Drive
Totowa, New Jersey, 07512

Printed in Hong Kong

British Library Cataloguing in Publication Data

Rose, Ellen Cronan
    The novels of Margaret Drabble.
    1. Drabble, Margaret – Criticism and interpretation
    I. Title
    823'.9'14   PR6054.R25Z/

MACMILLAN ISBN 0–333–28568–9

Barnes & Noble ISBN 0–389–20006–9

In gratitude, to the women of
Dartmouth College, especially
the University Seminar for
Feminist Inquiry

Contents

The illustration on page 127 is taken from R. L. Gregory's *The Intelligent Eye* (New York: McGraw-Hill, 1970), designed by E. G. Boring, and first published in the *American Journal of Psychology*, 1930.

Preface

This book was begun in the summer of 1977. Since then, I have incurred many debts. I would like here to attempt, however inadequately, to repay them, by thanking:

Cynthia Griffin Wolff, who started it all by asking "Why don't you write a book on Margaret Drabble?", who gave me a forum for many of the ideas I was working out in Chapter 2 by inviting me to speak on Drabble and Arnold Bennett at the 1978 session of The English Institute, and whose own high standards of scholarship have been a constant source of inspiration to me;

Jay Martin, who read and made many invaluable comments on the early chapters;

Carey Kaplan, Mort Levitt, Dee Preussner, Ann Rayson, and Kristina Valaitis, who have generously shared their thoughts and unpublished papers about Drabble with me;

The many participants in two panels on the fiction of Margaret Drabble – at the Modern Language Association in 1977 and at the Women and Society Symposium at St. Michael's College, Winooski, Vermont in 1979 – whose lively interest in Drabble's work helped keep mine alive;

The reference librarians of Dartmouth's Baker Library, especially Patricia Carter and Virginia Close, who tracked down fugitive items and delivered them, with a smile, to my desk;

The trustees of Dartmouth College, who granted me a Faculty Fellowship and time to write;

Mary Klages, for working through the de Beauvoir connection with me and for pointing out that the candy Janet Bird gives Connie Ollerenshaw is "Black Magic";

The University of Wisconsin Press for use of extracts from *Contemporary Literature*;

Claudia Card, for directing me to Mary Daly, Susan Griffin, and the witches, and for bringing champagne to celebrate the book's completion;

And most of all, Nancy Hayles, who was midwife to this labor.
Without her trenchant criticism there would be more errors than
there are; without her unfailing support there might not be a book.

E. C. R.

Acknowledgements

The author and publishers wish to thank the following copyright owners for permission to quote from the books of Margaret Drabble:

George Weidenfeld & Nicolson Ltd. and Alfred A. Knopf Inc. for extracts from *The Waterfall, The Needle's Eye, The Realms of Gold* and *The Ice Age.*

George Weidenfeld & Nicolson Ltd. for an extract from *Jerusalem the Golden*, and with William Morrow and Company Inc., for extracts from *The Garrick Year* and *The Millstone (Thank You All Very Much).*

Faber & Faber Ltd. and Alfred A. Knopf Inc. for two verses from 'Anecdote of the Jar' from *The Collected Poems of Wallace Stevens*, copyright 1923 and renewed 1951 by Wallace Stevens.

1 "The situation of being a woman": *A Summer Bird-Cage, The Garrick Year, The Millstone*

I

Margaret Drabble is a novelist because she is a woman. Had she been a man, she would no doubt have been an actor, since she did more acting than writing as an undergraduate at Cambridge in the fifties. After graduation, she joined the Royal Shakespeare Company, where she had a walk-on part in *A Midsummer Night's Dream* and understudied Vanessa Redgrave as Imogen in *Cymbeline*. She also had a baby, and discovered, as generations of women had before her, that "it rather cramped [her] style".[1] So she turned from acting to writing, since "women had never been shut off from the materials of fiction. A pencil and a piece of paper . . . and all human life was there".[2]

There are those who would question whether all of human life is there in Margaret Drabble's novels, at least in the early ones. For she is generally regarded not as a woman who writes novels but as a "women's novelist". This is a label she has recently been at some pains to shed.[3] But, like most labels, it can be useful if read correctly.

If a women's novelist is someone whose subject is women, then there can be no question, I think, that the author of *A Summer Bird-Cage, The Garrick Year*, and *The Millstone* was a women's novelist. Her subject was what it was like to be a woman in a world which calls woman the second sex. For whatever biological accident may have determined Margaret Drabble's choice of a career, the real impetus for her first novel was provided by a book she read during her last year at Cambridge, a book she acknowledges affected her profoundly, Simone de Beauvoir's *The Second Sex*. "This seemed to me to be wonderful material and so important to me as a person. It was material that nobody had used and I could use and nobody had ever used as far as I would use it".[4]

The Second Sex is an anatomy of what Drabble has called "the situation of being a woman" in a man's world. It polemically asserts that "one is not born, but rather becomes, a woman".[5] De Beauvoir describes "how woman undergoes her apprenticeship, how she experiences her situation, in what kind of universe she is confined, what modes of escape are vouchsafed her" (TSS, p. xxix). The crucial discovery a woman makes during her apprenticeship to life is that she *is* confined to a sphere created and ordained for her by men, and Drabble's early novels resound with this discovery. As she told one interviewer, "in my earlier novels I wrote about the situation of being a woman – being stuck with a baby, or having an illegitimate baby, or being stuck with a marriage where you couldn't have a job".[6]

But what a woman is really stuck with, in our culture, is the condition de Beauvoir describes as "alterity", which means that she is defined in relation to man. "Now, what peculiarly signalizes the situation of woman is that she – a free and autonomous being like all human creatures – nevertheless finds herself living in a world where men compel her to assume the status of the Other" (TSS, p. xxviii). In patriarchy, "humanity is male and man defines woman not in herself but as relative to him. . . . He is the Subject, he is the Absolute – she is the Other". Specifically, de Beauvoir says, man has decreed that woman is " 'the sex,' by which is meant that she appears essentially to the male as a sexual being. For him she is sex – absolute sex, no less" (TSS, p. xvi). And no more. Men "propose to stabilise her as [sexual] object and to doom her to immanence" (TSS, p. xxviii). Can a woman in this situation, de Beauvoir asks, become "an autonomous and transcendent subject" (TSS, p. 278)? Without employing – perhaps without even fully understanding – de Beauvoir's existentialist vocabulary, Margaret Drabble seems in her early novels to be exploring some of the practical implications of *The Second Sex*.

In 1969, an American interviewer asked Drabble whether she had "some sense of presenting a particular predicament, a particular kind of person" in her first novel, *A Summer Bird-Cage*. "Not really," she answered, "no. Though in fact, when I look at it, I can see now what the predicament was. I was in Cambridge last week and some girls in their last year came up to me and said, is it really so

awful when one leaves?"[7] It seems clear, in retrospect, that what
Margaret Drabble was doing in her first and perhaps her second
and third novels as well was "using" the "wonderful material" she
found in *The Second Sex* to try to understand the predicament girls
face when they leave what Sarah Bennett calls the "womb" of
college[8] – how and on whose terms to enter the adult world.

Sarah Bennett, of *A Summer Bird-Cage*, is the youngest of
Drabble's heroines. Just graduated from Oxford, with a first class
honours degree in English, she is on the verge of life, nervously
sniffing the future. At a cocktail party, someone asks her, "And
what will you be?" "How should I know?" Sarah replies, "I will be
what I become, I suppose" (SBC, p. 7). But her nonchalance is only
superficial. In fact, she thinks that this question, or problem, "was
the one thing that kept me strung together in occasionally ecstatic,
occasionally panic-stricken effort, day and night, year in, year out"
(SBC, p. 146).

According to Sarah, there are two answers to the question of what
to be. One is to be married to a don and the other, to be a don.
Marriage vs. career. Since her fiance, Francis, is studying for a year
in the United States, she is enjoying a kind of moratorium, exploring
both possibilities. None of the marriages she sees is encouraging.
One is happy but dull, another exhilarating but self-destructive,
and a third, her sister Louise's, in which she had hoped to find a
model for her own, ends in divorce. On the other hand, she seems to
have a natural bent of scholarship. Asked by her sister's lover
what she'd most like to achieve with her life, she says she'd like to
write a book (SBC, p. 196). And one of her reasons for despising
Louise's novelist husband is that he talks about novels "so professionally, whereas these things were life and death to me" (SBC,
p. 63).

Why then does Sarah decide, as she seems to have done by the end
of the novel, not to be a don, not to have a career? Here is her
explanation: "I'll tell you what's wrong with that. It's sex. You
can't be a sexy don. It's all right for men, being learned and
attractive, but for a woman it's a mistake" (SBC, p. 195). Virginia
K. Beards thinks that Sarah's "explanation as to why she will not
become a don indites everyone's absurd attitudes to the female out
of the kitchen or bedroom".[9] So it does. But it also indicates that
Sarah has internalized these attitudes. For Beards, Sarah's story
illustrates "the secondary status of the educated woman within
patriarchy". The primary focus of *A Summer Bird-Cage*, however, is

not the status within patriarchy of an educated young woman like Sarah, but her psychology.

"What will you be?" is a question usually asked of children, with or without the addition, "when you grow up". Sarah's real predicament is not the choice between marriage or a career (there is no reason offered why she couldn't combine them) but the more general predicament de Beauvoir describes in Chapter 8 of Volume II of *The Second Sex*, "The Young Girl". She must decide whether or not she wants to be a grownup woman in a society that calls women the second sex. Her problem is exacerbated by her unquestioning acceptance of patriarchy's definition of what it means to be a woman.

When Louise summons her home from Paris, where she has a job as a tutor, Sarah regards it as an order to stop wasting time (SBC, pp. 7–8). Her assignment, as she understands it, is to observe and learn from Louise, whose marriage signalizes to Sarah her sister's passage into adult womanhood.

Midway through the novel, Sarah makes a revealing disclaimer. "I meant to keep myself out of this story, which is a laugh, really, I agree; I see however that in failing to disclose certain facts I make myself out to be some sort of *voyeuse*, and I am too vain to leave anyone with the impression that the lives of others interest me more than my own" (SBC, p. 79). But precisely because she is so concerned with her own life, Sarah *is* a voyeuse. She is fascinated with the details of Louise's private life, her dirty underwear (SBC, p. 28), the interior of her closet (SBC, p. 140), and above all, her bedroom. Invited to a party at Louise and her husband's apartment, Sarah takes advantage of the suggestion that she leave her coat in the bedroom to "look round". Her gaze moves from the "white plaster frieze and cupids on the ceiling" to Louise's dressing table and cosmetics, and finally to "the big double bed". "Suddenly I felt rather guilty and inquisitive, sitting there in their bedroom and speculating on what they looked like in bed, as if I had been reading a diary instead of simply receiving unrejectable impressions . . ." (SBC, p. 129). When it turns out that Louise's sexual activity is not with her husband but with her lover, Sarah shifts her gaze to the affair, which she learns about "with a shock of inevitable familiarity. . . . Like children finding out about sex: they are shocked, surprised, and yet oddly certain that it must be so, because they have always known the unbelievable truth (SBC, pp. 100–101).

"Like children finding out about sex", observing or fantasizing the primal scene, Sarah has ambivalent feelings about adult sexuality. So long as she can merely observe it, she finds it irresistably desirable. But when she is invited to experience it, she becomes frightened. She thinks Louise's virile lover is "stunning" (SBC, p. 60). He is "huge and dark like a colossus" (SBC, p. 98). And when, at a party, he asks Sarah to dance with him she feels "dazed", "squashed", and "subdued" (SBC, pp. 98–99). She feels more comfortable with her own date, who kisses her arm "intermittently and absent-mindedly" (SBC, p. 101).

Sarah is obsessed with sex. She has fantasies of exhibiting herself: "tarty" dresses suit her, she would like to "strip things off" (p. 32), and she imagines herself exuding sex as her academic gown slips off her bare shoulders (SBC, p. 195). (Most people wear street clothes under their academic gowns.) But at the same time that Sarah is titillated by sex, she finds it terrifying. Exhibitionism may provoke rape. Perhaps all sexual contact is a form of rape or violation.

If Louise is Sarah's model of what it might mean to be married, her cousin Daphne is her model of the female don. And Sarah's description of Daphne, "a cross between a symbol and a cartoon" (SBC, p. 119), portrays her as the stereotypical old maid. "I have nice legs", Sarah reflects, "whereas Daphne's are muscular and shapeless round the ankles and covered in hairs and bluish pimples. Oh, the agony. If I had had any courage I would have told her to put on suntan stockings, but somehow I couldn't interfere with the awfulness of nature. It must be so frightful to have to put things on in order to look better, instead of to strip things off". Then engagingly, Sarah acknowledges that she's being a "bitch". The original Daphne, she remembers, "was chased by a god and was turned into a tree to preserve her virginity. Something our Daphne had preserved. Who would rape a tree?" (SBC, pp. 32–33).

However catty her description of Daphne may be, what Sarah sees in her is an equation of donnishness and sexlessness. And the nervous excess of her revulsion from Daphne suggests that, at some level, Sarah finds the "symbol" of the sexless, virginal don attractive. This suspicion is confirmed by Sarah's choice of a best friend, who – like Daphne – is a cross between a symbol and a cartoon. This mysterious friend, who never appears in the novel except through Sarah's reminiscences of her, is a kind of cartoon representation of Simone de Beauvoir, who wrote in *The Second Sex* that men have defined woman as " 'the sex', by which is meant that she appears essentially to the male as a sexual being". Sarah's friend, "gaunt Simone", with "her sexless passions" (SBC, p. 75), has refused this definition. Unique, defined in relation to no one but herself, she is autonomous; "nationless, sexless", she has transcended all external definition. "She doesn't belong anywhere", Sarah thinks. "Or perhaps she belongs everywhere. I'd like to be irresponsible like that. To be able to go on like that forever" (SBC, p. 53).

Sarah's attitude towards this symbolic cartoon character is much more complex than her attitude towards the relatively unattractive Daphne. Simone's letters "reassure and assert something in [Sarah] which is usually crying out for satisfaction" (SBC, p. 74), something in her that wants more than immunity from rape. What sex has got her married sister and friends is "kitchens and gas-meters and draughts under the door and tiresome quarrels" (SBC, p. 76). Like Simone, who gives Sarah "a sense of tradition and *salons* and Henry James" (SBC, p. 53), Sarah would like these things to have a "pure aesthetic value"; she would like "to force a unity from a quarrel, a high continuum from a sequence of defeats and petty disasters, to live on the level of the heart rather than the level of the slipping petticoat" (SBC, p. 219). Implicit in her admiration for Simone is her fear that losing her heart and her petticoat to a man dooms a woman to "immanence".

But if Sarah simply doesn't *want* to be "unsexy" like Daphne, she doesn't think she *can* be "sexless" like Simone, who is "cut after an unlivable pattern". Sarah loves and admires Simone for being "most purely personal in her life", but she is "vaguely aware of a hinterland of non-personal action" in herself, "where the pulls of sex and blood and society seem to drag [her] into unwilled motion" (SBC, p. 76).

In Sarah Bennett, Drabble has dramatized the situation of the young girl, as de Beauvoir describes it in *The Second Sex*. She "wishes to be a child no longer, but she does not accept becoming an adult" (TSS, p. 330) because "she enters adult life only in becoming a woman; she pays for her liberation [from parental authority] by an abdication [of her autonomy] (TSS, p. 341). The adolescent girl "cannot become 'grown-up' without accepting her femininity; and she knows already that her sex condemns her to a mutilated and fixed existence" (TSS, p. 306). For Sarah, growing up means accepting her sexuality, yielding to biological imperatives, "the pulls of sex and blood". As we have seen, sex frightens Sarah. Moreover, she does not want to be defined as a purely sexual being. She does not want to surrender her right to roam, as Simone does, "through a strange impermanent world where objects are invested with as much power as people, and places possibly with more" (SBC, p. 75), the world of the intellect and of art. But to remain in that world, which she and Simone knew at Oxford, "to go on like that forever", Sarah thinks she would have to remain an "irresponsible" child or become a "sexless" adult. And although sex frightens her, Sarah is convinced that "the world of sensations is where I live" (SBC, p. 75). Thus she is in the predicament de Beauvoir finds characteristic of the young girl: "she does not accept the destiny assigned to her by nature and by society; and yet she does not repudiate it completely". She is "divided against herself" (TSS, p. 330).

Perhaps the real explanation for Sarah's avid interest in her sister's marriage is that Louise intends "to have my cake and eat it"(SBC, p. 215), to combine marriage to a wealthy, sexually undemanding husband and a passionate affair with her glamorous, improvident lover. Given her sexual timidity, Sarah would probably not choose Louise's way of having her cake and eating it, but she does appropriate the metaphor in thinking of her own fiance: "respecting Francis I sometimes think I may be able to have my cake and eat it" (SBC, p. 105). "To force marriage into a mould of one's own, while still preserving the name of marriage – it seemed an enterprise worth consideration" (SBC, p.192).

In her study of *Eating Disorders*, the psychiatrist Hilde Bruch observes that many people "misuse the eating function in their efforts to solve or camouflage problems of living that to them appear otherwise insoluble. Food lends itself readily to such usage", she goes on, "because eating, from birth on, is always closely intermingled with interpersonal and emotional experience, and its physiological and psychological aspects cannot be strictly differentiated".[10] Sarah's ambivalence about growing up therefore quite logically, or psychologically, translates into a metaphor of eating, a desire to have her cake and eat it. In *A Summer Bird-Cage*, Drabble neither develops the implications of this metaphor nor gives her protagonist an eating neurosis. In her next novel, *The Garrick Year*, she does both.

In *A Summer Bird-Cage*, we see Louise Bennett's marriage through Sarah's eyes, as "an enterprise worth consideration". *The Garrick*

Year is an "anatomy"[11] of that marriage, or one very like it. At 26, Emma Evans is married to an actor named David and is the mother of two young children, Flora and Joseph. *The Garrick Year* is her narration of a season spent in Hereford, where David has taken a job in a new provincial repertory company. Emma resents leaving London and is bored in Hereford, so she determines to take a lover. Her choice is David's producer and director, Wyndham Farrar, who responds quickly to her flirtation and initiates a series of weekly clandestine meetings. Like Louise, Emma appears to be having her cake and eating it.

But Emma has not successfully resolved the conflict Sarah Bennett felt between her desire to become an adult woman and her wish to remain a child. And Drabble reveals this by describing Emma's odd eating habits and her unusual attitudes towards food and eating.

The Garrick Year opens with a cake which Emma neither has nor eats. Watching television, she sees Sophy Brent, an actress she had known in Hereford. "She was, typically enough, eating: She was advertising a new kind of chocolate cake, and the picture showed her in a shining kitchen gazing in rapture at this cake, then cutting a slice and raising it to her moist, curved, delightful lips. There the picture ended. It would not have done to show the public the crumbs and the chewing" (GY, p. 3). Is it the television camera which is fastidious? Or is it Emma?

At any rate, she is not like the greedy Sarah, who "loves" food and recalls with pleasure the "lovely meals" she has eaten. The one thing Sarah regrets about her bohemian life is that there are too few lovely meals; she envies Louise because she needn't worry about grocers' bills (SBC, p. 182). Emma, like Louise, dines out often, at others' expense. Yet she doesn't seem to take much pleasure in the lovely meals. Whereas Sarah eats and drinks heartily, Emma nibbles. She prefers *hors d'oeuvres* to steak and "fiddles" with her sole *Véronique* (GY, p. 145).

Emma spends a great deal of her time, when she is not dining out, preparing and serving meals to others. She is shown breast-feeding her baby, cooking lamb stew for lunch and spaghetti for her husband's friends, cutting bread-and-butter for tea, frying innumerable pans of bacon-and-eggs, whipping eggs for a mousse. But we seldom see her eating.

Nor does she take pleasure in seeing others eat. She regards her nursing infant as a "tiny, mousy, pathetic scrap of child" who "latched itself" onto her breast (GY, p. 8). And she is disgusted when Sophy comes to tea and eats "everything within sight, spreading far more jam on her bread than I ever think decent in company, dropping crumbs . . ." (GY, p. 100).

Emma is not uninterested in food. She is enough of a gourmet cook to make a chocolate mousse and she is particular, even finicky, about what she orders in restaurants. The hors d'oeuvres she prefers to entrées (GY, p. 164) are "avocado pears and prawn cocktails and artichokes" (GY, p. 195). On occasion, she even overeats. One night, stranded at home with the au pair girl in front of the TV, she eats "three helpings of chocolate mousse" (GY, p. 92).[12]

But such indulgence is rare, and Emma is in no danger of getting fat. Indeed, except for her breasts, which are abnormally large because she is nursing Joseph, she is "thin as a stick" (GY, p. 149). Her body is a "spiky" (GY, p. 188) collection of "bones and knobs" (GY, p. 196).

General abstinence from food, despite an intense interest and an occasional overindulgence in it, disgust with the act of eating, extreme thinness – these are the presenting symptoms of anorexia nervosa.[13]

In 1963, an Italian psychiatrist, Mara Selvini Palazzoli, published a book analyzing anorexia nervosa from a psychodynamic point of view.Her findings were corroborated in 1973 by Hilde Bruch, who believed that many women who "impress the casual observer and their friends and acquaintances as enviably slim, attractive, and interesting" reveal under psychiatric exploration "severe underlying psychopathology".[14] These women, no matter how normal and even attractive they look, behave like anorexics. Such a woman is Emma Evans.

The psychodynamic approach to anorexia nervosa sees the patient's attitudes toward food and eating as symbolic language. This is the language Emma speaks when she says she doesn't like steak. Once, dining out with Wyndham, she discovers that "there was nothing on the menu but steak and when the steak arrived it was the hugest piece I have ever seen, and it tasted distressingly of animal" (GY, p. 175). The size of the portion would daunt anyone determined not to gain weight. But why should the taste of beef "distress" Emma? As Wyndham observes, "most of you girls live on nice big steaks" (GY, p. 164).

Emma's associations, as she and Wyndham discuss the steak, reveal what it symbolizes for her. He, quite naturally, recalls boyhood visits to a cattle market. But Emma is "reminded of my own visits to nearby Cheltenham as a child, and how we used to go riding, as all middle-class girls go riding. We talked about this a little, and why girls should care so much more about horses than boys" (GY, p. 176). Emma's grammar is suggestively ambiguous. Do girls care more about horses than they care about boys? Or do girls care more than boys do about horses? Actually, girls do seem to care more about horses than boys do and often they seem to be more interested in horses than they are in boys. But as literature and art suggest (one need only recall D. H. Lawrence's *St. Mawr* or, on the more popular level, the motion picture *National Velvet*), to the adolescent girl horses can be powerful symbols of male sexuality. While seeming to ignore boys, she can express her inchoate sexual feelings in her devotion to her horse, without knowing that that is what she is doing. Emma's associations from steak to animal to horse invite the reader of *The Garrick Year* to make a further association from horse to sex and conclude that by rejecting steak, Emma is symbolically and unconsciously rejecting sex.

If in the restaurant Emma translates food into sex, in the bedroom she is likely to translate sex into food. When she and David move into their furnished flat in Hereford, Emma is appalled by the ugly furniture, particularly a wardrobe in the bedroom. David accuses her of being out of date:

> "That wardrobe, that's modern life. You'll just have to ram it down your gullet and swallow hard."
> As usual, the more grandiose of his statements managed to silence me. For it was modern life, that wardrobe, and I knew as I stared at it that I was going to do my best to swallow it; but I protested, nevertheless.

David continues:

> "And I'll tell you something else: I, like that wardrobe, am modern life. In its less desirable aspects. How far down your gullet do you think I've got?
> "You've stuck," I said. "You've stuck."
> "You mean I'm not digested?"
> "Not at all digested. You're all raw and whole and hairy" (GY, p. 52).

Emma not only finds David's body repugnant – she refuses even to kiss him after this argument, more often than not turns away from his sexual overtures ("I turned my own thin spine towards him", GY, p. 78) – there are more than a few suggestions that she is repelled by all physicality. She does not like "the mess of union" (GY, p. 24) that is marriage, she is "appalled by the filthy mess of pregnancy and birth" (GY, p. 32), and she is impatient to wean her baby because "my breasts were too big" (GY, p. 55). She habitually thinks of herself as a self divided, a "real" incorporeal self in opposition to a physical body, which is described as "rubbish". Recalling the moment when she first felt attracted to David, she says: "I myself, the surface of me, felt calm and dead and white in that unnatural glare, and the part of me that was not me, but just any old thing, the inside of me, the blood and muscle and water and skin and bone of me, the rubbish, was blazing away, shuddering like some augur's sacrifice" (GY, p. 28). Considering whether or not to enter into an affair with Wyndham Farrar, she uses almost the same language. "I wondered whether I was right to pay such attention to the part of me that responded with disturbing eagerness to the overtures of a man, like Wyndham Farrar, for what was it that responded in this way but the physical rubbish of me, the blood and skin and so forth . . ." (GY, p. 133).

These statements bear an uncanny resemblance to that made by one of Hilde Bruch's anorexic patients: "I have denied my body, I have pretended it did not exist, it was not worth anything. I did let it disintegrate as if 'myself' and 'it' were different – like two separate people. 'I' was in my body – but severed from 'it' – *I did not want what it stood for – to live like a mature woman.*"[15]

Long before Palazzoli described the psychodynamics of anorexia nervosa, doctors sensed that this eating disorder was psychogenic. Since the typical anorexic is a girl who looks like a boy, because she has starved away her feminine roundness, and who does not function biologically like a woman, because she does not menstruate, Janet, in 1903, "suggested that mental anorexia reflected the patient's refusal to play a feminine sexual role". With typically chauvinist elegance, Freud defined anorexia nervosa as "melancholia of the sexually immature".[16] Palazzoli, however, rejects "the old fable that anorexics are people who refuse to grow up and who reject their femininity". She believes, on the contrary, that what the anorexic's willful self-starvation shows "is a keen desire, however distorted, to become an autonomous adult".[17] The difficult task confronting the adolescent girl is to "realize her potential not only as an individual, but as a distinct and unique person who assents to her existence, that is to her own body and sex".[18] In other words, she must become an autonomous adult who is also an embodied woman.

At this point, Margaret Drabble cannot imagine what such a woman might be like. Instead she gives us in Emma Evans the pathological but logical extension of what de Beauvoir regards as the normal situation of the young girl. She "feels that her body is getting away from her, it is no longer the straightforward expression of her individuality; it becomes foreign to her; and at the same time she becomes for others a thing: on the street men follow her with their eyes and comment on her anatomy. She would like to be invisible; it frightens her to become flesh and to show her flesh" (TSS, p. 288).[19] Unable to assent to her own body and sex, Emma dreams of Julian, the young homosexual actor in David's company:

> I dreamed, seemingly all night, of Julian. It was an extraordinary dream, clearer than some of life itself. We were walking through Islington, Julian and I, and we were passionately in love. Islington itself was not the place I know it to be, but the place it must once have been, with wide grass walks and fields and dandelions growing in the paving stones. It was as green as it now is stony, and I felt for Julian all that I had ever felt for anyone. I can remember it so distinctly, that image of breathless, exhausting, total admiring love. We had our arms round each other, and I could even imagine in my dream what his thin girl's body would feel like to hold, so different from Wyndham's solid trunk or David's muscular torso; we were walking northwards from the Angel, towards Islington Green, and when we got there we sat down on one of the benches that bears the inscription "Persons are not allowed to sleep on this seat," and there we froze together in some immobile trance amongst the buttercups and the meadowsweet. It was like a scene out of a book, a passion out of a poem, it had all the pure intensity that never occurs in life, the dizzy undistractedness, with no rivers, no children (GY, pp. 202–203).

This dream fulfills Sarah Bennett's wish "to live on the level of the heart rather than the level of the slipping petticoat". "Like a scene

out of a book, a passion out of a poem, it [has] all the pure intensity
that never occurs in life". "The main issue" for the anorexic, Hilde
Bruch says, "is a struggle for control".[20] Staying slim is "proof of her
power to defy nature".[21] Defying nature, Emma's dream constructs
an Eden in Islington.

Ellen Moers believes that landscapes, which frequently have
"nothing to do with the plot of the novel",[22] figure in many novels
written by women as metaphors for female sexuality. Emma's
fantasy of sexless love occurs in a frozen tableau, "with no rivers".
Asked by Nancy Hardin whether she had a symbolic intention with
the water imagery in several of her novels, including *The Garrick
Year*, Margaret Drabble gave a matter-of-fact explanation for the
emphasis in that novel on water and drowning: "*The Garrick Year*
was about a year we spent in Stratford-on-Avon with the Royal
Shakespeare Company. The River Avon is very dangerous; while
we were there at least two people were drowned . . . I realized
halfway through the book that drowning was what was going on
and therefore at the end it would be most suitable if Julian drowned
himself". But why Julian? The answer points to a symbolic meaning
of water and the natural landscape which Drabble may not want to
talk about, but which is nonetheless demonstrably present in *The
Garrick Year*. It also points out Emma's anorexic determination to
defy nature.

Emma's initial attraction to her future husband was not to his
"personal attributes" which she "rather disliked", but to something
in him which inspired in her "a feeling of terror". "With him, I felt
that I was on the verge of some unknown and frightful land, black
desert, white sand, huge rocky landscapes, great jungles of ferns
(GY, p. 29).This landscape, which has nothing to do with the plot of
the novel, is psychic; what Emma feels "on the verge of" is her own
sexuality and the part of her which responds to it is her "guts",
which she would like to disavow as "rubbish". Later, confronting
the possibility of an affair with Wyndham Farrar, "my guts sagged
or stiffened or drooped, I am not sure what they do, but they do it
from intense fear or apprehension or memory" (GY, p. 112). The
memory Wyndham activates is clearly of the response her guts made
to David, and the fear is of yielding to her own sexuality.

Towards the end of the Garrick Year, Emma's small daughter
falls into the Wye. This real event in a real landscape assumes
symbolic meaning when Emma remembers a song:

Mother, may I go out to swim,
O yes, my darling daughter,
O yes, you may go out to swim,
But don't go near the water (GY, p. 198).

Don't go near the water, don't get wet "with milk and blood and tears, a varied sea of grief" (GY, p. 190), with the wetness that is the essence of female sexuality – the blood of menstruation, the lubricity of the ready vagina, the broken sac of amniotic fluid.

On the symbolic level, then, to drown means to yield, to assent to, one's own sexuality. Julian drowns himself, in part, because the "strain" of deciding whether or not to "give in" to the advances of another male actor "proved too much for him". His drowning thus represents his tacit acceptance of his homosexuality. But Emma will not accept her sexuality: "You will not find me at the bottom of any river. I have grown into the earth, I am terrestrial" (GY, p. 219).

Like Sarah Bennett, Emma Evans wants adulthood on her own terms. She wants marriage, but she does not want to fulfill her conjugal obligations. She wants motherhood, but she doesn't want to breast-feed. And she wants sexuality, but only from the waist up: "Kissing I did not mind: in fact, I soon discovered that anything above the waist, so to speak, I did not mind, but anything below was out of the question" (GY, pp. 164–165). Although she would not use the metaphor, she too wants to have her cake and eat it.

But just as Sarah Bennett does and does not want to grow up, Emma both does and does not want to be grown up. Looking back over her abortive affair with Wyndham, she reflects: "Somewhere I had gone wrong . . . I had not faced the choice that I should faced . . ." (GY, p. 212). She had not confronted the possibility that her guts might not be rubbish, but the "dark and wanting" (GY, p. 133) aspect of her self, a "hungry bony bird who was ready from some unexplained famine to eat straw and twigs and paper" (GY, p. 116.)

At the end of The Garrick Year, Emma is still married, having apparently succeeded in forcing marriage into a mould which both she and her husband find sufficiently comfortable. She is also, however, still a divided self, vigorously asserting that she is made not of flesh but of "cast iron" (GY, p. 218). Four years later, Drabble will return to see what has become of this married, divided woman. Then she will call her Jane Gray and her novel The Waterfall. But for the time being, she turns her attention to the other option Sarah

Bennett was contemplating. In her next novel, *The Millstone*, she considers what it might be like to be a sexless, virginal female don.

2

Rosamund Stacey must be unique among contemporary fictional women, whose odysseys are routed from bed to bed. Her relationships with men follow a pattern begun with a college boyfriend named Hamish, a particular version of having her cake and eating it in which she appears to be having an affair while actually abstaining from sex. Although she and Hamish spend nights together, in college and in hotel rooms, they do not make love. "In those days, at that age," Rosamund reflects, "such things seemed possible and permissible".[23] But after Hamish, she cannot find a lover so compliant to her unorthodox requirements, so she devises an elaborate strategem for gratifying her needs, "an excellent system, which combined, I considered, fairness to others, with the maximum possible benefit to myself" (M, p. 18). She dates two men simultaneously, giving each to understand that she is sleeping with the other. What Joe and Roger get from this arrangement is hard to say; what Rosamund gets is what she wants and all she can tolerate. "The one thing I could not dispense with was company", she says. "All I had to sacrifice was interest and love. I could do without these things".

"Touch without contact" (M, p. 28) is what Rosamund wants, and because she believes George Matthews, whom she thinks is homosexual,[24] may be able to give her this, she allows him to make love to her and thus becomes pregnant. Her unique sexual encounter is not a moment of communion or even of communication. It is accidental and incidental to Rosamund's real concerns, which are with her graduate research and her prospective career as that female don Sarah Bennett decided not to be. In fact, it becomes apparent very early in *The Millstone* that what she names "the Hamish pattern" is not simply her "suspicion, [her] fear, [her] apprehensive terror of the very idea of sex" (M, p. 17). What Rosamund is actually rejecting is one of the consequences of sex, intimate involvement with another human being. It is love she is rejecting, not sex, as is clear in her response to Joe's desire to help her through her pregnancy, whoever the father may be. "All I knew was that I must get rid of Joe quick, before he sensed my poverty, because Joe was capable of pity and kindness" (M, p. 38).

Rosamund's poverty is spiritual, a result of her inability to accept love. And she knows it. Contemplating the birth of her child, she thinks:

> Hitherto in my life I had most successfully avoided the bond that links man to man, though I had paid it some lip service . . . I was never fool enough to think that one can get something for nothing; I knew one had to pay one's way and I considered that I had paid mine by the wit of my conversation, by a certain inherited prestige, by having a nice flat for parties, and by possessing a fine pair of legs. . . . [But] although I recognized the principle of payment, I had some basic deficiency when it came to taking appropriate goods in exchange (M, p. 59).

Much later, she reflects that "if I asked more favours of people, I would find people more kind" (M, p. 134).

What compels Rosamund to ask a favour, she "who could not even ask for love or friendship" (M, p. 61), is her obligation to her daughter, Octavia. Because she cannot leave her baby unattended while she runs an errand, she must ask the neighbors to keep an eye on her. During her pregnancy, Rosamund has inklings that becoming a mother will necessarily involve her with other human beings: "I saw that from now on I . . . was going to have to ask for help, and from strangers too"(M, p. 61). Pregnancy makes her see that "I was trapped in a human limit for the first time in my life, and I was going to have to learn how to live inside it"(M, p. 50). Nevertheless, she tries to avoid the lesson. Like Emma, she prides herself on her ability to put mind over matter, to control her body. She is working in the British Museum when it dawns on her that she is pregnant. She stops working long enough to check dates on her pocket calendar, "which was difficult as I never make a note of anything, let alone of trivial things like the workings of my guts" (M, p. 30).[25] When she is convinced, finally, that she is pregnant, her mind goes blank. Understandably, her predicament has driven Elizabethan poetry out of her head. But Rosamund will not let her body have the last say. Like an anorexic in this regard, if not in her eating habits, she "turns her back on the existentially inevitable, on everything that is imposed by, and inherent in, her corporeality".[26] She returns to the poems of Sir Walter Raleigh and "by the end of the morning I had covered exactly as much ground as I had planned. It gave me much satisfaction, this fact. Much self-satisfaction" (M, p. 31).

She continues throughout her pregnancy to find satisfaction in going on with her work. Far from impeding her thesis, her condition gives her an excuse to sever most of her social contacts and work more hours, so that she thinks she may even "finish my thesis before the baby" (M, p. 76). She sees "no reason why [her] proposed career of thesis, assistant lectureship, lectureship and so on should be interrupted" (M, p. 43) by having a baby. "I simply did not believe that the handicap of one small illegitimate baby would make a scrap of difference to my career" (M, p. 94), she says, and apparently she is right. By the end of the novel, her thesis has been published, she has been offered a post "at one of the most attractive new universities" (M, p. 129), and she is "embarked on a piece of work on Cowley" and "a chapter in a paperback survey of poetry". She thinks, with a degree of self-satisfaction that verges on smugness, that Dr. Rosamund Stacey is "a form of address which would go a long way towards obviating the anomaly of Octavia's existence" (M, p. 129). Nancy Hardin believes that all this goes to show that "Rosamund Stacey is basically a competent and self-reliant young woman scholar",[27] but like Marion Vlastos Libby, I find Rosamund's accomplishments "rather chilling".[28]

What begins to break down the walls of Rosamund's prison is, as she herself foresaw, becoming a mother. For although, like Emma, she does not like the mess of mothering (she quickly gives up breast-feeding because, for one thing, she "grew frantic at the way [her] clothes got covered with milk", M, p. 96), on the whole it gives her profound pleasure. In fact, the closest Rosamund comes to sensual pleasure is in giving birth. In the final throes of labour, she feels "sensations which though unbelievably violent were now no longer painful but indeed almost a promise of pleasure" (M, p. 85). After she delivers, she lies awake, resisting the sleeping pills she has been given, "unable to get over [her] happiness". "I was not much used to feeling happiness: satisfaction, perhaps, or triumph, and at times excitement and exhilaration. But happiness was something I had not gone in for for a long time, and it was very nice, too nice to waste in sleep" (M, p. 87).

Of course, being a mother is not unalloyed happiness. And Rosamund is given a larger quotient of pain than most mothers are assigned: Octavia is discovered to have a congenital heart defect (which – the literary Rosamund might, but doesn't, reflect – is a kind of poetic justice).

But although Rosamund is poignantly aware of the ordeal surgery must be for an infant who has never been separated from her mother, although she uncharacteristically throws a temper tantrum in order to gain admittance to Octavia's room because "somewhere Octavia was lying around and waiting for me" (M, p. 110), her feeling for her baby is not "intense and very beautiful", as Libby believes. It is intense, but it is not beautiful, because it is not feeling for another person, no matter how much Rosamund and most of her critics may believe it is. Trying to describe what she feels when she first holds her baby, Rosamund settles for "love, I suppose one might call it, and the first of my life" (M, p. 86). But what she loves is a "small living extension of myself" (M, p. 123). And the intense pain she undeniably experiences during the weeks preceding Octavia's surgery is tinged with resentment:

> Now for the first time I felt dread on another's behalf, and I found it insupportable. . . . As I emerged from each fit of grief, I felt bitter resentment against Octavia and against the fate that had thus exposed me; up to this point, I had been thoroughly defended and protected against such onslaughts, but now I knew myself to be vulnerable, tender, naked, an easy target for the malice of chance (M, p. 101).

Rosamund's first, and logical, response to the discovery that she is pregnant is to have an abortion. But, knowing more of books than of the world, she bungles her several attempts. Later, she wonders whether it wasn't something like fate that determined she should carry the child to term. "The more I thought about it, the more convinced I became that my state must have some meaning, that it must, however haphazard and unexpected and unasked, be connected to some sequence, to some significant development of my life" (M, p. 57). Although this interpretation of the situation is childishly narcissistic, it contains a grain of truth. For becoming a mother does offer Rosamund an opportunity to break down the walls of her isolation and connect, lovingly and vulnerably, with another.

If becoming a mother were a significant development in Rosamund's life, it would affect her relationship not only with Octavia, but with people in general. There is no sign, however, that

Rosamund is significantly nearer the possibility of true intimacy at the end of *The Millstone* than she is at the beginning of the novel.

When she discovers that she is pregnant, Rosamund wonders whether to tell George. Her decision not to is based on her fear of exposure (M, p. 31). If she tells him he is the father of her baby, she may at the same time destroy his "image of [her] own imaginary wickedness" (M, p. 21). After Octavia is born, Rosamund thinks for a moment that perhaps she ought to tell George about her, so that he could enjoy her as Rosamund does. But she doesn't, ostensibly because "no amount of [Octavia's] charm could possibly balance the quite unjustified sense of obligation, financial, personal, and emotional, that such a revelation would instantly set to work. So I spared him and myself" (M, p. 97). She may well be sparing herself, but has she any right to "spare" George the knowledge of his paternity? Isn't he entitled to the sense of obligation, as well as to the sense of pleasure, which parenthood affords Rosamund and which she selfishly claims as her sole property?

So long as it is a matter of seeking George out to tell him of his paternity, Rosamund's failure to share the obligation of parenthood is only a sin of omission. But, by a coincidence as unlikely as the one which resulted in her pregnancy, she meets George in an all night drugstore and invites him back for a drink and a look at her baby:

> "You've got a baby, have you," said George. "I didn't even know you were married."
> "I'm not," I said, and smiled, this time with true confidence; for here I was, safely back in my old role, the girl with alternating lovers, the girl with stray babies, the girl who does what she wants and does not suffer for it" (M, p. 136).

Back in her shell, in other words. The scene with George in her flat, which ends *The Millstone*, is a retreat on Rosamund's part from communication, communion, and love. Whenever George makes an attempt to get through to her, she adds another layer of bricks to her enclosure. The first indication that George is still interested in Rosamund is, of course, his coming over to speak to her at the chemist's. As we have seen, Rosamund both beckons him, by inviting him home, and holds him at a distance, by misrepresenting herself as a sexual vagabond. When George responds "in his most camp tones" (M, p. 136), Rosamund is satisfied; now she feels him "so little a threat" that she "[feels] weak with relief".

George is interested enough in Rosamund to have read her articles, which can only be found in scholarly journals which are not lying around in dentists' waiting rooms. He wants to know when her parents are coming back, how sick the baby has been, "everything, everything" (M, p. 140) about her. But she witholds information, even lies to keep him from knowing the truth. She wishes they could "sit there forever estranged, forever connected",[29] but knows "that a connection so tenuous could not last, could not remain frozen and entranced forever, but must melt if so left, from the mere mortal warmth of continuing life. If one of us did not move towards the other, then we could only move apart" (M, p. 140).

George, like Octavia, is an invitation to Rosamund to be human, and Rosamund knows it: "I felt myself on the verge of tears[30] and noise, and I held hard onto the arms of my chair to prevent myself from throwing myself on my knees in front of him, to beseech from him his affection, his tolerance, his pity, anything that would keep him there with me, and save me from being so much alone with my income tax forms, from lacking him so much. Words kept forming inside my head, into phrases like I love you, George, don't leave me, George. I wondered what would happen if I let one of them out into the air. I wondered how much damage it would do" (M, p. 141).

What could possibly be damaged? Decorum? Pride? On the other hand, what might possibly be gained? An end to solitude, true intimacy, the sharing of responsibility for Octavia.

"If one of us did not move towards the other, then we could only move apart". It is George who moves. Not knowing that Octavia is his, being a bachelor unused to babies, George is understandably uninterested in Rosamund's invitation to view her sleeping child. But he does, and says, "She's beautiful".

> "Yes, isn't she?" I said.
> But it was these words of apparent agreement that measured our hopeless distance, for he had spoken for my sake and I because it was the truth. Love had isolated me more securely than fear, habit or indifference. There was one thing in the world that I knew about, and that one thing [sic] was Octavia. I had lost the taste for half-knowledge. George, I could see, knew nothing with such certainty (M, p. 143).

It is not love that isolates Rosamund. George's "She's beautiful" is a loving statement because it is spoken for Rosamund's sake. Her agreement is not a loving statement, but simply a statement of fact. She does not love Octavia – she knows her. Loving is risky, but Rosamund has no taste for uncertainty.

I have discussed the concluding pages of *The Millstone* at some length because my reading of the novel differs from the one that generally prevails. Not only most critics but most women readers I have talked to believe that Rosamund Stacey has achieved that desirable feminist synthesis Sarah Bennett aspired to: that by remaining single she has established her independence, while through her motherhood she has affirmed both her flesh and her bonds with humanity. Nancy Hardin asserts that "as a result of Rosamund's commitment to her pregnancy and subsequently to Octavia, she achieves a true synthesis both within herself and with the outside world". And Virginia Beards celebrates *The Millstone* as marking "a growth in the author's feminist consciousness" because "Rosamund successfully defines herself in relation to values other than the male-superiority/female-dependency ones of patriarchy".

But since, as Valerie Myer notes, Rosamund is "incapable of sharing Octavia with George, of extending her love to anyone but Octavia",[31] since I have argued that she does not even love Octavia except as an extension of herself, being a mother does not link her with the outside world. And whether or not *The Millstone* marks the growth of Drabble's feminist consciousness, Rosamund is no feminist heroine. She does *not* define herself in relation to non-patriarchal values. Like the fathers, she is "successful" because she puts mind over matter.[32] She is as divided a self as Emma Evans.

We do not know how Sarah Bennett's dark, sexless friend Simone felt about herself. But when the equally gaunt Emma Evans looks in a mirror, she sees "an unattractive, dark-skinned, spiky misfit", who in another age "could at the best have hoped to be a bluestocking or a pillar of the Church" (GY, p. 188). And at one point in *The Millstone*, the bluestocking Rosamund reflects that it is "unnerving . . . to see oneself for a moment as others see one, like a glimpse of unexpected profile in an unfamiliar combination of mirrors" (M, p. 82). Rosamund does not often look into such mirrors, but Drabble seems to have placed a couple of them in the novel for the reader's benefit. A letter from Rosamund's sister Beatrice is one of them. Rosamund had written her that she was pregnant, and Beatrice's response is worth quoting at length, because it represents a reaction to Rosamund's predicament which is reasonable, sympathetic, and notably absent from Rosamund's own deliberations about what to do:

> I must say you didn't go into many details about the whole thing, but from what you said I gathered you were intending to keep the child. I feel I must tell you that I think this is the most dreadful mistake, and would be frightful for both you and the child – just think, if you had it adopted you could forget about the whole business in six months and carry on exactly where you left off. . . . I just can't see you adapting yourself to the demands it would make on you, you've always been so set on your independence and having your own way. . . . However, it isn't just you that I'm thinking of. It would be bad enough for you but it would be far, far worse for the child. Through no fault of its own it would have to have the slur of illegitimacy all its life, and I can't tell you how odiously cruel and vicious children can be to each other, once they get hold of something like that. A baby isn't just something you can have just because you feel you ought (M, pp. 66–67).

This letter says some good things about Beatrice. First, that she knows her sister very well, knows that raising a child would conflict with Rosamund's taste for solitude and independence. Second, that she loves her and wants to do all she can to see that Rosamund will not make a decision which could make her permanently unhappy. Third, and most important, that she thinks about the child as a person who will have to live out the consequences of Rosamund's decision. "A baby isn't just something you can have just because you feel you ought".

But this is precisely what Rosamund decides to do. Beatrice's letter makes her angry because "nobody had the faintest right to offer me any advice about my own child. . . . [her letter] revealed to me the depth of my determination to keep the baby. The determination at this stage cannot have been based, as it later was, on love, for a I felt no love and little hope of feeling it; it was based rather on an extraordinary confidence in myself, in a conviction, quite irrational, that no adoptive parents could ever be as excellent as I myself would be" (M, pp. 67–68). I have already questioned whether, even "later on", Rosamund truly loves Octavia. However that may be, consideration of the child's welfare plays almost no role in her decision to have it and keep it.

Another mirror which shows us Rosamund as she really is is her friend Lydia's novel. One evening, Rosamund chances upon the manuscript of the novel her flat-mate is writing and realizes, after the first few pages, that she is its subject and protagonist. For the first few pages, she is pleased with Lydia's portrait of herself: "I emerged rather well – independent, strong-willed, and very worldly and *au fait* with sexual problems". She is less happy with Lydia's hint, "subtle enough technically", that "the Rosamund character's obsession with scholarly detail and discovery was nothing more or less than an escape route, an attempt to evade the personal crisis of her life and the realities of life in general" (M, p. 79).

This glimpse that the reader gets into Lydia's unfinished novel may be Drabble's hint, subtle enough technically to evade most readers of *The Millstone*, that Rosamund's independence, competence, and self-reliance are not positive attributes, but attempts to avoid acknowledging her existential vulnerability, her need for other people and her responsibilities to them.

But while I believe that Beatrice's letter and Lydia's novel may be invitations by Drabble to step outside Rosamund's point of view, they are not sufficiently compelling or authoritative. Bernard Bergonzi, for instance, agrees with Rosamund that Lydia's novel contains "copious distortions and misrepresentations".[33] And many readers think Beatrice is self-righteous and insensitive (certainly her statement that if Rosamund puts her baby up for adoption she will be able to "forget about the whole business in six months" is insensitive.)

This brings us to the central problem raised by Drabble's first three novels. I have grouped them together for discussion because they seem to belong together: *A Summer Bird-Cage* states a problem and *The Garrick Year* and *The Millstone* offer alternative solutions to it. But they also belong together because they are the only of Margaret Drabble's novels written wholly in the first person. What makes these novels so interesting, even if the reader is not so eager as Drabble to consider the predicament young women face as they enter adulthood, is their intriguing and often perplexing mixture of the exemplary and the personal.

When she was asked whether she was "working out [her] own problems" in her first three novels, Drabble answered evasively: "It's almost inevitable, I think, that one should write about one's own age group and the preoccupations of it".[34] But Sarah, Emma, and Rosamund seem to be more than simply fictional members of

Drabble's "own age group"; they resemble their creator in certain very detailed ways. Sarah and Rosamund are Oxbridge English majors like Drabble and like her they have important and complex relationships with their sisters.[35] *The Garrick Year* is clearly based on a year Drabble and her husband spent in Stratford-upon-Avon. And the predicament which generated and which runs through all three novels is the predicament Drabble found herself in at the conclusion of her undergraduate career, "twenty-one, free, unemployed, wondering where to go, watching my friends and contemporaries to see where they would go".[36] Especially since all three novels are narrated in the first person, it is hard to know when the protagonists are personae of Margaret Drabble and when they are simply intended to represent members of her own age group. More importantly, it is difficult to know how objectively she views Sarah Bennett's "predicament" and Emma Evans' and Rosamund Stacey's alternative "solutions" to it.

For example, I have described Emma Evans as neurotic, a divided self whose behaviour exhibits her ambivalence about sexuality and her desperate struggle to assert and preserve her identity. But Drabble described Emma to one interviewer as "strong".[37] Is she aware that this strong woman has an almost pathological problem with sexuality? Recalling that revealing conversation in the bedroom, where Emma's aversion to sex revealed itself in eating imagery, I have to note that it was not Emma but Drabble who introduced that imagery into the conversation, by way of David.

Valerie Myer thinks that Drabble takes the "risk" in these novels that "imperceptive readers will take the characters' views for those of the author".[38] She sees this as a technical problem, a risk inherent in the use of first-person narration. And indeed, first-person narration often creates problems for both the reader and the novelist. To what extent are we meant to rely on the narrator, to accept her evaluations of other characters and of the events of her history? If we are not meant to rely on her, how can Drabble let us know that we are not supposed to? I think Drabble is experimenting in *The Millstone* with ways of introducing other, often critical, points of view into first-person narration. But the remarkable lack of critical consensus about how to "read" the character of Rosamund Stacey indicates at the very least that it is difficult for Drabble to convey the nuances of her characterization to the reader, using the first-person narrational mode.

But the problem of "placing" Drabble's first three heroines may be more than technical. I think this technical problem may manifest a more profound difficulty Drabble was having in achieving sufficient detachment from the experience she shared with other women of her own age group to analyze and understand it.

NOTES

¹ From Nancy S. Hardin, "An interview with Margaret Drabble", *Contemporary Literature*, Vol. 14, No. 3 (Summer 1973), 273–295.
² Interview with Terry Coleman, "A Biographer Waylaid by Novels", *Guardian*, 106 (April 15, 1972), 23.
³ See especially her interview with Mel Gussow, "Margaret Drabble: A Double Life", *The New York Times Book Review* (October, 9, 1977), pp. 7, 40–41.
⁴ "Margaret Drabble", in *The Writer's Place: Interviews on the Literary Situation in Contemporary Britain*, ed. Peter Firchow (Minneapolis: University of Minnesota Press, 1974), pp.102–121.
⁵ Simone de Beauvoir, *The Second Sex*, trans. H. M. Parshley (New York: Alfred A. Knopf, 1953), p. 249. Further references to TSS will appear in the text.
⁶ Interview with Nancy Poland, "Margaret Drabble: 'There Must Be a Lot of People Like Me' ", *Midwest Quarterly*, Vol. XVI, No. 3 (Spring 1975), 255–267.
⁷ Firchow, op. cit.
⁸ Margaret Drabble, *A Summer Bird-Cage* (1962; rpt. New York: Belmont Books, 1971), p. 197. Further references to SBC will appear in the text.
⁹ Virginia K. Beards, "Margaret Drabble: Novels of a Cautious Feminist", *Critique*, Vol. 15, No. 1 (1973), 35–47.
¹⁰ Hilde Bruch, *Eating Disorders: Obesity, Anorexia Nervosa, and the Person Within* New York: Basic Books, 1973), p.3.
¹¹ Margaret Drabble, *The Garrick Year* (1964; rpt. New York: Morrow, 1965), p. 23. Further references to GY will appear in the text.
¹² As Jay Martin pointed out to me, this is *h'ors d'oeuvres* at the other end of the meal. She is still avoiding the *entrée*.
¹³ Of the two eating disorders Hilde Bruch has studied, anorexia nervosa is much less common than obesity. Although some older women and a few men exhibit the syndrome, it is usually manifested in adolescent girls, who suddenly and unaccountably stop eating. For years, anorexia was diagnosed when certain somatic conditions obtained: the patient had suffered an extreme loss of weight (from 25 to 50 pounds), was amenorrhoeic, constipated, and hyperactive. In recent years, however, attention has shifted to the etiology of the disease.
¹⁴ Bruch, op. cit., p. 207.
¹⁵ Ibid., p. 279.
¹⁶ Quoted in Mara Selvini Palazzoli, *Self-Starvation* (1963), trans. Arnold Pomerans (London: Human Context Books, 1974), p. 9. Even Bliss and Branch, whose monograph is the standard discussion of the disease in somatic terms, conclude that "when one reviews [the patients'] histories it is impressive to note how ill-prepared they were as a group to meet the vicissitudes of adulthood. The

majority seemed to lack the emotional substructure necessary to healthy, rewarding interpersonal relationships. Many were not ready for responsibility or independence and were not equipped to adapt well to marriage, parenthood, or sexuality". They conclude that "severe reduction of weight then becomes a neurotic, unrealistic way to return to former years". Eugene L. Bliss, M. D. and C. H. Hardin Branch, M. D., *Anorexia Nervosa* (New York: Paul B. Hoeber, 1960), pp. 48, 60.

[17] Palazzoli, op. cit., p. 72.

[18] Ibid., p. 77.

[19] Palazzoli explains why a girl becomes anorexic in terms an existentialist would find familiar. The changes a girl's body undergo during puberty frighten her for two reasons. First, they remind her that she is biologically doomed to play a passive-receptive role. And second, there seems to be nothing she can do about it; her body's "indiscreet and uncontrollable development makes her look upon [it] as an irresistible intruder, that is, as part of the external environment". In short, her body becomes her enemy. It is also perceived by the potential anorexic as the one part of the external environment over which she *can* exert control. Ibid., pp. 70–72.

[20] Bruch, op. cit., p. 251.

[21] Ibid., p. 104.

[22] Ellen Moers, *Literary Women: The Great Writers* (New York: Anchor Books, 1977), p. 387.

[23] Margaret Drabble, *The Millstone* (1965; rpt. as *Thank You All Very Much*, New York: New American Library, 1969), p. 8. Further references to M will appear in the text.

[24] Rosamund's night with George is Emma's Julian dream come true.

[25] And like Emma, she chooses an ugly and derogatory word to describe her body and its functions.

[26] Palazzoli, op. cit., p. 81.

[27] Nancy S. Hardin, "Drabble's *The Millstone*: A Fable for Our Times", *Critique*, Vol. 15, No. 1 (1973), 22–34.

[28] Marion Vlastos Libby, "Fate and Feminism in the Novels of Margaret Drabble", *Contemporary Literature*, Vol. 16, No. 2(Spring 1975), 175–192.

[29] Cf. Emma's wish – and her language – in her dream of Julian.

[30] Again there is a verbal echo from *The Garrick Year*, where Emma similarly felt "on the verge" of acknowledging her sexual and human vulnerability.

[31] Valerie Grosvenor Myer, *Margaret Drabble: Puritanism and Permissiveness* (New York: Barnes and Noble, 1974), p. 175.

[32] As Rosemary Ruether points out, the "alienation of the masculine from the feminine" which de Beauvoir named as the "primary sexual symbolism" of patriarchy "sums up" all the "basic dualities" of patriarchy – "the alienation of the mind from the body; the alienation of the subjective self from the objective world; the subjective retreat of the individual, alienated from the social community; the domination or rejection of nature by spirit". See her "Motherearth and the Megamachine: A Theology of Liberation in a Feminine, Somatic and Ecological Perspective", in *Womanspirit Rising: A Feminist Reader in Religion*, ed. Carol P. Christ and Judith Plaskow (New York: Harper Forum Books, 1979), p. 44.

[33] Bernard Bergonzi, *The Situation of the Novel* (London: Macmillan, 1970), p. 204.

[34] Firchow, op. cit.
[35] For an intriguing insight into the possible complexities of the Drabble sisters' relationship, one should read Antonia (Drabble) Byatt's novel, *The Game* (New York: Scribners, 1967).
[36] Interview with Barbara Milton, "Margaret Drabble: The Art of Fiction LXX", *The Paris Review*, No. 74 (Fall-Winter 1978), 40–65.
[37] Hardin interview, op. cit.
[38] Myer, op. cit., p. 176.

2 "An appreciation of Bennett":*Jerusalem the Golden*

In her biography of Arnold Bennett, Margaret Drabble says that Bennett never considered using the Potteries as the subject of fiction until he read George Moore's *A Mummer's Wife*, "which opened [his] eyes to the romantic nature of the district [he] had blindly inhabited for over twenty years".[1] Bennett, she conjectures, "needed the distance of art to make the reality tolerable and malleable". Between her third and fourth novels, Drabble herself made a number of discoveries: that in her first three novels she had been blindly inhabiting the district of her own experience; that in order to make that reality malleable as fiction, she would need to distance herself from it; and that art – particularly the art of Arnold Bennett – would make that possible.

Jerusalem the Golden is Margaret Drabble's first wholly realized novel, economical in its construction, finely precise in its characterization of the heroine. In later novels she will be more profound; never will she be more completely in control of her material than in this relatively early work.

This control is all the more impressive when we realize that *Jerusalem the Golden* is if anything even more candidly autobiographical than its predecessors. In her biography of Bennett, Drabble says she based the novel on her childhood memories of Sheffield: "I wrote the book from memory" (AB, p. 5). Like Drabble, the heroine of *Jerusalem the Golden* grows up in the "barren territory"[2] of the industrial north of England. Her mother is both dour and self-righteous, or as Drabble has said of her own mother, depressed and depressing.[3] Not surprisingly then, Clara views winning a scholarship to London University (as Drabble may have anticipated going to Cambridge) as her chance to escape to "some less obstinately alien world" (JG, p. 73). In her final year at the university she finds that and more, "a truly terrestrial paradise, where beautiful people in beautiful houses spoke of beautiful things" (JG, p. 37). She meets, in short, the Denhams, a large, colourful, eccentric, affectionate family, the antithesis of her own.

In her interview with Drabble, Nancy Hardin observed:

A significant characteristic of the young women in your novels is their inability to accept the values of their parents. Instead, they commit themselves to a search for "chosen" or "extended" families (friends, lovers, or perhaps children) with whom they work through their identities and beliefs. Clara Maugham of *Jerusalem the Golden* comes to mind.

Drabble's response is revealing:

I've often wondered whether this is a problem that is particular to me in any way, or whether it's a problem that afflicts almost all girls, and men too – that one has to escape from one's own family and find substitute families or substitute patterns of living. I don't know whether this might well reveal my own feeling about my own family background. For many years my mother was very depressed. She's now not, thanks to, well quite frankly, thanks to drugs. So throughout my adolescence I was struggling with the fact that adult life seemed to be incredibly depressing . . . One had to find some image of liveliness or color or love that was different from what one had been brought up on. I don't know how I would have developed if I'd known my mother as she is now. She is so much more cheerful and active. I might have had a completely different view of needing to leave the family or having to find other mother figures. But I certainly do – did, I think – look for other mother figures . . . What one is looking for is just patterns of living in other people.

Clara finds not only patterns of living in the Denhams' house but a lover too, in their married second son, Gabriel. At another point in the Hardin interview Drabble said:

I don't know why one gets married. I was completely enchanted by [my husband's] whole family life, which was so unlike my own. And in a way I'm still enchanted by them. I find it a terrible trial, but at the same time I can't get away from it since he left. We separated about a year ago and I see more of them since than ever before.

Unlike Drabble and her husband, Clara and her lover do not separate. And at the end of *Jerusalem the Golden*, Drabble departs further from autobiography to imagine Clara called back to Northam to tend her dying mother. She chooses not to stay there, but to consign her mother to the doctors and return to "a bright and peopled world, thick with starry inhabitants, where there was no ending, no parting, but an eternal vast incessant rearrangement" (JG, p. 252).

Despite this fairy-tale ending, in *Jerusalem the Golden* Drabble is clearly working with what she has called "aspects of me".[4] Yet in Clara Maugham, she has so successfully objectified these aspects of herself that Clara achieves an independent existence, a life of her own about whose imaginary future her creator can only speculate: "She's going to turn into something fearsome, I think. I rather dread her future".[5]

2

In order to make his memories both tolerable and malleable, Arnold Bennett needed, so Drabble supposes, distance from them. So too in *Jerusalem the Golden* does she distance herself from certain aspects of herself, initially and most simply by writing at 27 a novel about a 22 year old. More importantly, of course, she achieves distance as she says Bennett did, through art.

The art which informs *Jerusalem the Golden* is of two sorts. The first is a complex system of allusions to other literary works, by which Drabble objectifies her protagonist and makes subtle judgments about certain of the supporting characters, chiefly the Denhams.[6] The second is a density of language in the descriptive and narrative portions of the novel: images of colour and vegetation are developed as a running commentary on the action and on the moral development of Clara Maugham.What makes both sorts of artistry possible is an almost ridiculously simple expedient, a shift from the first-person narrative perspective of the early novels to limited third-person narration.

In 1966, Drabble published a short story which is of little interest except as an exercise in third-person narration. As such, it reveals a novice's ineptitude. "Hassan's Tower"[7] is narrated in the third person, but it is totally limited to the point of view of one of its two characters. Moreover, the narrator has not just limited her omniscience to this character's point of view, she has adopted it, simply recording and reporting his impressions.

Drabble's next use of third-person narration is considerably more flexible and expressive than in "Hassan's Tower". In *Jerusalem the Golden* she exploits one feature of the technique she had ignored in that story: that is, the narrator, even when restricted to Clara's point of view, is not Clara herself. This enables Drabble to make the narrator's language characterize Clara, revealing things about her which she either does not know or would not want to reveal.[8]

Furthermore, in *Jerusalem the Golden*, the narrator moves freely from Clara's point of view to her lover's, thus providing a complex and satisfyingly ambiguous characterization of her heroine, who is seen not only subjectively – from inside her own head, and objectively – in terms of her behaviour, but intersubjectively – as her behaviour affects Gabriel, whom we know and come to like.[9]

Jerusalem the Golden is more artful than its predecessors in more ways than in its manipulation of narrative perspective. Using third-person narration gives Drabble the possibility of using language more poetically than she had previously. In contemporary, colloquial monologue (the linguistic medium of Drabble's first three novels), one seldom finds recurring images or extended metaphors. In the more impersonal prose of *Jerusalem the Golden* there are both. Drabble uses light imagery, for instance, to define Clara's aspirations and then undercuts them by associating with the dominant light imagery a verbal motif of coinage, which underscores Clara's ruthlessness in the pursuit of her golden dream.[10]

In short, Drabble is in greater control of her material in this artful novel than she was in its relatively artless predecessors. And by exercising this control, she achieves fictional objectification of a character derived from certain aspects of herself and ironic distance from her.

But what aspects of herself? And how did she gain artistic perspective on them? To answer both questions we must return to Cambridge, where Drabble was not only "profoundly affected" by reading Simone de Beauvoir but profoundly engaged in writing "her solid Eng. Lit. project"[11] on Arnold Bennett, whose surname she gave to her first heroine. Antedating Drabble's appreciative and affectionate biography of Bennett by seven years, *Jerusalem the Golden* demonstrates that his influence on her was at least as profound as de Beauvoir's if not more so.

We don't know much about Sarah Bennett's home in Warwickshire, only that she hates it. But some of that unexplored hatred and her equally unexplored dislike for her nagging mother may account for her envy of her friend Simone, who is "nationless" and whose parents are dead. We do know, thanks to Nancy Hardin's interview, that Margaret Drabble was eager to leave Sheffield and her mother. Thus it is reasonable to assume that when she read in *The Second Sex* that "sovereign freedom" is an "authentic demand" for an individual to make (TSS, p. 278), she may have translated de Beauvoir's existentialist language into words that met her existential need to break free from her family and home.

"Freedom" is a slippery concept. It can mean freedom *from* external constraints, and certainly it has that meaning in *The Second Sex*. But as de Beauvoir uses it, "freedom" – or the word she prefers, "autonomy" – means primarily freedom *to* transcend biological and other limitations by affirming one's imagination and creativity.

I see no evidence in Drabble's early novels that she defines freedom in this affirmative sense. Sarah Bennett simply does not want to be tied down to "kitchens and gas-meters and draughts under the door". She envies her friend Simone for "that succession of journeys and train tickets which is [her] life" (SBC, p. 74). This character is a caricature of Simone de Beauvoir. But maybe Drabble didn't know it.

If we assume that Simone is an incarnation of what Drabble understood by freedom, then we may see in Sarah's ambivalence about her friend Drabble's own suspicion that such freedom is neither possible nor wholly desirable. Sarah suspects that Simone's way of life is "irresponsible", and Drabble suggests that Emma Evans and Rosamund Stacey achieve what measure of freedom they do by failing to respond to and be responsible for other human beings.

Clara Maugham is a full-blown portrait of the cartoon Drabble sketched in *A Summer Bird-Cage* of a Simone character. Unlike Sarah Bennett, she has no doubts that freedom is desirable. Hating and yet fearing her home town and her mother, "because she doubted her

power to escape" (JG, p. 30), Clara has by the end of the novel
succeeded in escaping both and looks forward to a future in which
there are no ties, no obligations, in which human relationships will
be "shifting and ideal conjunctions . . . like the constellations in the
heavens" (JG, p. 252). But Drabble puts her in a plot where this
happy ending is inappropriate, a plot modelled on at least two and,
I will suggest, probably three of Arnold Bennett's novels.

Drabble begins the third chapter of her biography of Bennett
with the following admission:

> I should acknowledge at this point my own debt to Bennett, in my
> novel *Jerusalem the Golden* . . . . The girl in *Jerusalem the Golden* like
> Bennett's first hero [Richard Larch, in *A Man From the North*], is
> obsessed with escape, and she too is enraptured by trains and
> hotels and travelling: she feels she has "a rightful place upon the
> departure platform" of her home town. There is a good deal of
> Hilda Lessways in her too, for like Hilda she relished adventure
> and irregularity, and like Hilda she is summoned to her mother's
> death bed by telegram and does not respond in quite the right
> spirit. Perhaps it is irrelevant to mention these matters, but to me
> they are so much bound up together that my novel is almost as
> much an appreciation of Bennett as this book is meant to be (AB,
> pp. 47–48).

This far from irrelevant statement allows me to suggest that
Bennett's novels served Drabble as Moore's *A Mummer's Wife* had
earlier served Bennett: they gave her a perspective from which to see
the fictional possibilities of one aspect of her youthful attraction to
the philosophy of Simone de Beauvoir. Drabble's statement of
indebtedness to Bennett further suggests that she achieved distance
from this remembered aspect of herself by a formal manoeuvre.
Putting a Simone character in a Bennett plot shows her up as the
"spiky misfit" part of Drabble suspected all through her first three
novels she really was.

The plot that Drabble borrowed from Bennett has been described
as follows by Jerome Hamilton Buckley:

> A child of some sensibility grows up in the country or in a
> provincial town, where he finds constraints, social and in-
> tellectual, placed upon the free imagination. His family, es-
> pecially his father, proves doggedly hostile to his creative instincts

or flights of fancy, antagonistic to his ambitions, and quite impervious to the new ideas he has gained from unprescribed reading. His first schooling, even if not totally inadequate, may be frustrating insofar as it may suggest options not available to him in his present setting. He therefore, sometimes at a quite early age, leaves the repressive atmosphere of home (and also the relative innocence), to make his way independently in the city (in the English novels, usually London). There his real "education" begins, not only his preparation for a career but also – and often more importantly – his direct experience of urban life. The latter involves at least two love affairs or sexual encounters, one debasing, one exalting, and demands that in this respect and others the hero reappraise his values. By the time he has decided, after painful soul-searching, the sort of accommodation to the modern world he can honestly make, he has left his adolescence behind and entered upon his maturity. His initiation complete, he may then visit his old home, to demonstrate by his presence the degree of his success or the wisdom of his choice.

Bennett followed these "broad outlines of a typical *Bildungsroman* plot"[12] in writing both *A Man From the North* and *Clayhanger*; substituting the feminine for the masculine pronoun and "mother" for "father", this outline also serves to describe the plots of *Hilda Lessways* and *Jerusalem the Golden*.[13] By reverting in *Jerusalem the Golden* to this essentially male pattern of development, Drabble may implicitly be rejecting the argument of *The Second Sex*, that women face unique problems in growing up and that their development, therefore, has a pattern of its own. More importantly, she is explicitly adopting certain conventions of the genre which define what constitutes growth and maturity. In the typical *Bildungsroman*, as Buckley points out, the hero attains maturity through a process of inner growth which demands constantly that he reappraise his values. It is this inner growth which distinguishes him from a character type who resembles him in almost every other respect, the picaro.

Like the *Bildungsroman*, Robert Alter reminds us, "picaresque literature is very much a literature of learning". But unlike the *Bildungsheld*, the picaro does not change as a result of what he learns:

Whenever we encounter him, the picaroon appears as a fixed personality who never substantially alters during the course of his varied experiences. He learns, but he does not change. In the early chapters of a picaresque novel, the young hero is generally made to undergo some sort of *déniaisement* or "wising-up" . . . This same ritual of initiation is practiced in the novels of Balzac, Stendhal, and in the *Bildungsroman* in general, but in these works it is the first step in a process of serious inner development. The picaroon, on the other hand, once he has learned all the rules of the game . . . goes on to play with skill and confidence, but nothing has happened to him inside, no development has taken place.[14]

We meet Clara Maugham as a child, calculating how she may advance herself or, to use her word, "progress". She proceeds to educate herself, to acquire the knowledge, tastes, and opinions which will enable her to make her way in the sophisticated world to which she aspires. Friends, teachers, boyfriends are valuable to her insofar and only insofar as they can teach her what she thinks she needs to know in order to play the game she wants to play. And at the end of the novel, she congratulates herself that she *has* advanced, "oh yes, without doubt" (JG, p. 250).

But in her progress[15] Clara carefully avoids any lessons that may truly educate her, that may cause her to call into question her narrowly selfish goal.[16] Thus Drabble establishes that she is not a *Bildungsheld* but a *picara*. But by placing her in the typical *Bildungsroman* plot, Drabble suggests that her refusal to learn from her experience, to reappraise her values, is a shortcoming rather than a virtue.

Drabble borrows from Bennett's novels not only what Buckley calls the broad outlines of a typical *Bildungsroman* plot, but – as her statement in the biography indicates – episodes and character prototypes. She even uses in *Jerusalem the Golden* some of the specific language of these "parent novels", a phrase she invented to describe Bennett's own use of *Eugénie Grandet* in writing *Anna of the Five Towns* (AB, p. 95).[17]

Not all readers of *Jerusalem the Golden*, of course, will recognize its many allusions to *A Man From the North*, *Clayhanger*, and *Hilda Lessways*. But the reader who does know Bennett's novels will see that this extended allusion to Bennett's three *Bildungsromane* was extremely important to Drabble. By playing off her heroine against her literary prototypes, she was able, for the first time, "to refashion the personal so that it [could] stand entirely separate from her".[18]

In *A Feast of Words: The Triumph of Edith Wharton*, Cynthia Griffin Wolff says that Wharton achieved distance from herself in her first novel, *The Valley of Decision*, by responding "antiphonally" to Stendhal's *The Charterhouse of Parma*. Antiphony, she says, served Wharton "principally as a mechanism for placing her fictional world in a suitable, larger context – definitively distinct from self".[19] This is precisely the mechanism by which Drabble achieved in *Jerusalem the Golden* what she had been struggling to achieve in her first three novels, and it can best be illustrated by comparing *Jerusalem the Golden* with one of its parent novels. In the Bennett biography, Drabble calls attention to similarities between Clara Maugham and Hilda Lessways: "like Hilda [Clara] relished adventure and irregularity, and like Hilda she is summoned to her mother's death bed by telegram and does not respond in quite the right spirit". But just as Bennett's Anna "is not simply Eugénie rewritten in English terms" (AB, p. 95), *Jerusalem the Golden* is not simply an updated *Hilda Lessways*. Drabble's statement in the biography misleadingly suggests parallels between the novels which do not exist. Clara and Hilda are alike in their relish for adventure and irregularity, but their stories end very differently. Drabble alters the prototypical plot of *Hilda Lessways*, allows Clara to play a variation on the Hilda theme, and thus sees and clearly shows the reader how inferior a human being Clara Maugham is.

Raised by her mother to assume a sense of responsibility, Hilda struggles during her adolescence to assert her irresponsibility, to doff the apron of domesticity in favour of the printer's smock, to enter the man's world. When her mother, motivated by *her* sense of responsibility, goes to London to help her old friend Sarah Gailey set up a lodging house, Hilda "tasted her freedom to the point of ecstasy".[20] She throws herself into her work correcting proofs at the newspaper office and is so busy getting out the first edition that she waits 24 hours to respond to Sarah Gailey's telegram: "Mother ill. Can you came?" (HL, p. 146). When, on her tardy arrival in London, she discovers that her mother has died, she is overwhelmed with guilt and suffers what the doctor calls a nervous breakdown. But Hilda knows better:

> She knew, profoundly and fatally, the evil principle which had conquered her so completely that she had no power left with which to fight it. This evil principle was Sin. . . . She was the

Sinner, convicted and self-convicted. . . . she existed in the chill
and stricken desolation of incommutable doom (HL, p. 181).

From that point on, Hilda is the prisoner of her fate. She assumes her
mother's responsibility for Sarah Gailey and knows, however much
she may be dazzled by "the far vista of the hours which she had
spent with the Orgreaves [her Denhams]", that she will never be
able to enter that charmed circle, except as an infrequent visitor.
"The vision was like that of another and quite separate life. Would
she ever go back to it? . . . It seemed to her fantastic, impossible,
that she should ever go back. It seemed to her that she was netted by
destiny" (HL, p. 307).

For Clara, as for Hilda, freedom is desirable. More than
anything, she wants to be free from her mother. Varying the plot of
Hilda Lessways, Drabble does not give Clara a taste of freedom by
sending Mrs. Maugham to London. Instead she sends Clara to
Paris, where she has a week of dizzying freedom: "she felt free, the
light weight of her limbs, the clear grey spaces in her head, the
ebbing of her need, these were merely the symptoms of her
freedom" (JG, p. 230).

On her return to London, however, she finds a telegram sent days
before, summoning her to Northam, where her mother is seriously
ill. Her response to the telegram echoes both Hilda's sense of guilt
and her fatalism: "She stood there, staring at the fatal yellow paper,
and her first thought was, I have killed my mother . . . And she felt
closing in upon her, relentlessly, the hard and narrow clutch of
retribution, those iron fingers which she had tried, to wilfully, so
desperately to elude; a whole system was after her, and she the final
victim, the last sacrifice, the shuddering product merely of her past"
(JG, p. 234).

But Clara's mother, unlike Hilda's, is not dead. By departing
from the prototypical plot of Hilda Lessways, Drabble offers her
heroine the happy ending Bennett withheld from his, a way of
avoiding what Hilda calls her "incommutable doom" and Clara
rephrases as "the hard and narrow clutch of retribution". She is
free, as the last chapter of *Jerusalem the Golden* opens, to make what
she will of the opportunity Drabble is about to give her.

As an adolescent, Clara needed an antagonist in order to assert
her unique identity. She thinks of her environment in general terms
as hostile, but specifically she casts her mother as her antagonist. For

that reason, "the worst moments of Clara's domestic life were not in fact those moments at which domestic indifference fronted her most blankly and sheerly, for they could be faced by an equally stony frontage – they were those which bore witness to hidden chinks and faults deep within the structure" (JG, pp. 67–78). One such moment is the one in which Mrs. Maugham, stepping out of the character Clara has assigned her, gives her daughter permission to go on the school trip to Paris. Clara is not only disconcerted, but dismayed by her mother's generosity:

> Because the truth was that this evidence of care and tenderness was harder to bear than any neglect, for it threw into question the whole basis of their lives together. Perhaps there was hope, perhaps all was not harsh antipathy, perhaps a better daughter might have found a way to soften such a mother. . . . And who, having heard impartially this interchange, would have believed in Clara's cause? Clara's one solace had been the cold, tight, dignity of her case, and this had been stolen from her, robbed from her by an elderly woman's few words of casual humanity. She had learned a fine way of sustaining the role of deprivation, but gratitude was an emotion beyond her range (JG, pp. 70–71).

Now, years later, Clara is given an opportunity to extend the range of her emotions, to stop being an adolescent rebel. Once again she is brought face to face with "the hidden chinks and faults, deep within the structure" of her mother's character, which Clara had wilfully insisted was as grim and impregnable as granite.

Waiting to visit her mother in the hospital, Clara discovers a cache of old photographs and exercise books that date from before Mrs. Maugham's marriage. In the photographs, Clara sees on her mother's face "a smile radiant with hope and intimacy" (JG, p. 239). Reading the notebooks, she learns that, like her, her mother had once dreamed of "a brighter world/Where darkness plays not part" (JG, p. 240).

Recognizing her kinship with this woman, Clara goes to bed with "a sense of shocked relief", feeling "for the first time, the satisfaction of her true descent" (JG, p. 241). But the satisfaction, and the lesson, do not last. The next day, when Clara visits her mother in the hospital, she finds she cannot speak to her as "to that young woman" in the photograph taken "forty years ago". Clara thinks it would go "against nature", but she is wrong. "I did not know that a pattern forms before we are aware of it, and that what we think we make becomes a rigid prison making us. In ignorance and innocence I built my own confines, and by the time I was old enough to know what I had done, there was no longer time to undo it". These words of Rosamund Stacey's (M, p. 9) perfectly describe Clara's situation. She is not free, because she is a prisoner of her own will, which she nurtured on antagonism. In her mother's hospital room, she reenacts the anxiety of her adolescence:

> She found herself watching anxiously, fearfully, for any sign of feeling [on her mother's part], for any chink in the stony front, because it was in truth the last thing that she wanted, the last thing that she could have borne. And there was nothing, nothing at all; with relief she saw that there would be nothing, that she would not be called upon to give, that she could merely answer meanness with meanness (JG, p. 245).

Abandoning her mother to return to London, Clara gives up the possibility of true freedom, the ability to act creatively. Her declaration of independence, which concludes the novel, is an ironic revelation of how securely she is a prisoner of the fate she has created for herself: "Her mother was dying, but she herself would survive it, she would survive because she had willed herself to survive, because she did not have it in her to die. Even the mercy and kindness of destiny she would survive; they would not get her that way, they would not get her at all" (JG, p. 253).

Jerusalem the Golden was written in 1967, the centenary of Arnold Bennett's birth. And on May 11 of that year, Margaret Drabble published in the *Observer* a preview[21] of her biography of Bennett, which did not finally appear until 1974. When it did, it bore the following gold monogram on its cover: *MD · AB*. The suspended dot between the two sets of initials is like a mathematical symbol connoting relationship. The book avows that relationship and offers tantalizing clues for adumbrating it.

Drabble's first reason for wanting to write a biography of Bennett, she says, is that she "very much admired Arnold Bennett as a writer" (AB, p. xi). This admiration is apparent in her extended and perceptive discussions of Bennett's novels in the biography and in her own fiction as well, which she as well as a number of her critics has placed in the Bennett tradition. "I don't want to write an experimental novel to be read by people in fifty years, who will say, ah, well, yes, she foresaw what was coming", Drabble declared in a 1967 BBC interview. "I'd rather be at the end of a dying tradition, which I admire, than at the beginning of a tradition which I deplore".[22]

But one does not write a biography primarily to record one's appreciation of the subject's accomplishments; even a literary biography is an account of a life, and Drabble acknowledges that her "admiration for Bennett as a man, and not only as a writer, was also considerable" (AB, p. xi). Leon Edel has suggested "that if someone were to attempt to study the psychology of biographers, he would discover that they are usually impelled by deeply personal reasons to the writing of a given life".[23] Drabble confirms his hunch by revealing, on the second page of her biography of Bennett, her real reason for writing it: "What interests me more [than his career] is Bennett's background, his childhood and origins, for they are very similar to my own. . . . So, like all books, this has been partly an act of self-exploration" (AB, p. xii). I have been suggesting that *Jerusalem the Golden* too is "an act of self-exploration", and I believe that Drabble was helped in performing that act by the example of Arnold Bennett, the man as well as the writer.

Reviewing Drabble's biography of Bennett, Roger Sale says that "Arnold Bennett . . . is someone I have always felt warmly about; so too is Margaret Drabble, though I hadn't realized until now that perhaps the sources of these warm feelings were similar. Bennett was from Stoke-on-Trent, Drabble is from Sheffield, and while both eagerly left home and never wished to return, Bennett in his major novels and Drabble (in part by her reading of those novels) realized the hold these industrial Midlands cities still had on them".[24]

Looking at Arnold Bennett, Drabble would see a man like herself, with Simone's desire for freedom, a man "born in the Potteries, [who] spent the rest of his life trying to escape".[25] She would see him projecting his fears that he might not succeed onto fictional alter egos – Richard Larch, Edwin Clayhanger, and Hilda Lessways – who fail to escape the fate determined for them by their heredity and environment. In these novels Drabble finds "speculation about one's other self, about the self one might have been had a degree of determination or talent or luck not intervened" (AB, p. 174).

Looking at Bennett, Drabble would also see a man who wrote two sorts of novel, escapist fantasies like *The Grand Babylon Hotel*, *Hugo*, and *Imperial Palace*, and realistic novels like *Clayhanger* and *The Old Wives' Tale*. She would easily see which was better. And she would draw the only possible conclusion: that however understandable it may be to want to escape one's "background, childhood, and origins", success in that endeavour means artistic impoverishment. His best novels are those in which, spiritually, Arnold Bennett comes home:

> In *Clayhanger*, Bennett pays his debt to the world which he escaped so narrowly. Born himself into a relentlessly aspiring family, he himself aspired. . . . He removed himself, in spirit and in body, as far as he could from his origins. But writing in Fontainebleau, or in the luxury hotel in Brighton, he still feels his kinship with those left behind, in time and in place. . . . He describes them with a poetry as fine as Zola's (AB, p. 176).

In a finely perceptive aside, Drabble notes that another man from the north, D. H. Lawrence, wrote one of his own novels as "an ironic and critical commentary on *The Old Wives' Tale* or *Anna of the Five Towns*". Like Sophia and Anna, the heroine of *The Lost Girl* "is the daughter of a draper, and she too makes her escape from the drab, ruined world of the Midlands into a new country, in her case the mountains of Italy. Lawrence said of Bennett: 'I hate Bennett's resignation. Tragedy ought really to be a great kick at misery. But *Anna of the Five Towns* seems like an acceptance' ". Drabble's dry comment shows how little she thinks of Lawrence's "great kick": "Sophia endures and Anna endures, whereas Lawrence's heroine escapes . . ." (AB, p. 253).

"We are not free from our past, we are never free of the claims of others, and we ought to not wish to be".[26] This is the lesson Drabble read in the novels of Arnold Bennett she most admired. It is a lesson she would find corroborated in his life. In *Jerusalem the Golden*, even more than in the biography, Drabble records her "appreciation" to Arnold Bennett for teaching her this lesson. In *Jerusalem the Golden*, Drabble seems consciously to have done what Bennett had done in his three *Bildungsromane*. She speculates about her other self, the self who wanted freedom, as Bennett wanted to escape the Potteries. And with a fine irony she names her Clara, "after a Wesleyan great aunt" (JG, p. 5) named Hamps, "one of the most vital, dreadful, awe-inspiring women in English fiction" (AB, p. 27). Modelling her heroine in other respects on Bennett's *Bildungshelden*, Drabble allows her to succeed in realizing her and their and Bennett's and Drabble's fantasy of escape – and then exposes the poverty of that fantasy. *Jerusalem the Golden* is for Drabble what she says *A Man From the North* was for Bennett: "a projecting of fears, a confronting of the worst. And by writing it, by finishing it and publishing it, [Drabble] ensured that the worst would never happen to [her]" (AB, p. 67). Never again in her fiction will she entertain the idea that freedom from responsibility is either possible or desirable.

But she will begin to explore an idea she glimpsed briefly and perhaps for the first time in writing the concluding chapter of *Jerusalem the Golden*, that freedom, in de Beauvoir's sense of "autonomy", is entirely compatible with responsibility to and for other people. For what enslaves Clara Maugham is not her obligation to her mother, but her refusal of that obligation and the opportunity for self-knowledge and creativity accepting it might have afforded her. In her next novel, Drabble will discover what real freedom is all about.

NOTES

1. Margaret Drabble, *Arnold Bennett* (New York: Alfred A. Knopf, 1974), p. 2. Further references to AB will appear in the text.
2. Margaret Drabble, *Jerusalem the Golden* (1967; rpt. New York: Popular Library, 1977), p. 30. Further references to JG will appear in the text. As a reviewer in *The New York Times Book Review* observed when *Jerusalem the Golden* was published, the book contains "misprints galore", which apparently have never been corrected in subsequent reprintings. In quoting from the novel, I have quietly corrected obvious misspellings and mispunctuations.
3. Hardin interview, op. cit.
4. Ibid.
5. Ibid.
6. Consider, for instance, how she suggests that there is something sinister about the "radiant intimacy" of the Denhams' family life.

    Clara "had never in her life seen or heard of such a mother . . . nor had she ever seen an image of fraternal love. She had read of it, in the classics, as she had read of human sacrifices and necrophilia and incest, but she had not thought to see it with her own eyes" (JG, p. 131). What the reader is invited to see, in Clara's unaccountable reference to human sacrifice, necrophilia, and incest, is that there is something very unnatural indeed about the Denham menage. Invited to come meet Annunciata before she leaves for Oxford, Clara wonders "what it must be like to have relatives that one could thus serve up" (JG, p. 138), and the reader, remembering human sacrifice, thinks of Thyestes' gruesome banquet. Seeing Annunciata and Clelia together, Clara reflects that "her acquaintances in Northam . . . would have considered such affection unnatural, and probably perverted". So does the reader, when Clara then thinks, "unaccountably, of Christina Rossetti's Goblin Market".

In her brilliant analysis of Goblin Market (*Literary Women*, pp. 153–161), Ellen Moers shows that this "best-loved Victorian poem" is in fact a revelation of "the erotic life of children". What it reveals to Moers is the "night side of the Victorian nursery", in which incest between brother and sister and between sister and sister may have occurred as often in fact as in fantasy. In a moment of candour and intimacy, Gabriel says to Clara, "I could spend the rest of my life with Clelia; I miss her. I've never said this to anyone before, not even I think to myself, but it's true, I miss her, when I married I began to miss her. . . . If she *weren't* my sister, I would miss her, and since she is, why should I not?" Clara answers, "If she weren't your sister, you would probably have married her" (JG, pp. 209–210), and at another point she says to him, "All your family always seem to me to be in love with all the rest of your family. If you see what I mean: it always seems to be life with incest, don't you think?" (JG, p. 208). But Clara, who "had always been strangely compelled by the passionate and erotic relationship described in [Goblin Market]" (JG, p. 143), is not put off by the strong odour of perversion that clings to the Denhams. Rather, she elects to join the family and share its life of incest.

7 Margaret Drabble, "Hassan's Tower", in *Winter's Tales* 12, ed. A. D. Maclean (London: Macmillan, 1966), pp. 41–59.

8 The effect of this aspect of limited third-person narration is evident in the first sentence of the novel, whose latent ironies are almost as rich as those of the famous, and similar, sentence which opens *Emma*: "Clara never failed to be astonished by the extraordinary felicity of her own name". In *A Summer Bird-Cage*, that sentence would have read, "I never fail to be astonished by the extraordinary felicity of my own name", and it would have indicated not only the heroine's narcissism but her disarming confession of it. Spoken about Clara, rather than by her, this sentence suggests that she is vain and self-centred, but does not encourage us to suppose that she admits or even acknowledges that she is.

9 In chapter seven, the narrator frees herself from Clara's point of view to tell us things about Gabriel's and his wife Phillipa's experience which Clara may not know, since the narrator has told us that Clara "tried to piece together, from what she saw, the rest of Gabriel's life: but she tried idly, luxuriously, because she did not really want to know. She did not want to know everything about him" (JG, p. 190). What the reader learns makes her sympathize with Gabriel. Married to a neurotic, frigid woman, Gabriel endures the unhappiness of living with her because "he thought that she needed him" (JG, p. 177). Thus he is not only an unhappy man, but a good one, and we appreciate the ambivalence he feels about initiating an affair with Clara, who "seemed to him, in his ignorance, to be everything that Phillipa was not: warm, enthusiastic, easily amused, amusing, and wonderfully, mercifully unexhausted" (JG, p. 171).

Of course "in his ignorance" is the narrator's reminder to the reader that Gabriel is wrong, that some of the qualities he perceives in Clara are not there. What is missing is warmth, as we discover when, after nine pages of narration from Gabriel's point of view, the narrator shifts back to Clara's:

Gabriel wrote to Clara. She had not known what to expect from him, hardly daring to fear that there might be nothing, and when it was a letter that she received she knew that there could have been nothing more satisfactory (JG, p. 179).

"Satisfactory". That one word is enough to tell us what we will discover later in the novel, that Clara finds "more pleasure in the situation [of having an affair] than in the man" (JG, p. 197).

[10] Again, we may turn to the first sentence of the novel for an instance: "Clara never failed to be astonished by the extraordinary felicity of her own name". For our purposes, the extraordinary felicity of Clara's name is that it derives from the Latin *clarus*, meaning light or brightness.

Throughout the novel, Clara looks for an alternative to what she perceives as her colourless, drab home. As a child, her favourite hymn was "Jerusalem the Golden", which made her think "not [of] the pearly gates and crystal walls and golden towers of some heavenly city, but [of] some truly terrestrial paradise, where beautiful people in beautiful houses spoke of beautiful things". In her youth, "all people who were not from Northam seemed at first sight equally brilliant, surrounded as they were by a confusing blur of bright indistinct charm" (JG, p. 8). And her first glimpse of what becomes for her that terrestrial paradise she had imagined as a child *is* blurred and confused: on her first visit to the Denhams' house, "she did not know where first to look, so dazzling and amazing were the objects and vistas and arrangements before her" (JG, p. 117).

As Clara becomes acclimated to the Denhams' house and way of life, she compares their drawing room, where people sit "irradiated from behind by some small gold local source of light" to the Maughams' sitting room in Northam, where "all the light fell brightly in the small square bow-fronted room, from one central plastic-shaded bulb" (JG, p. 154). But while she admires the Denhams' house with its "gilt-framed" armchairs, "gold" mirrors, "gilt" candle-brackets, "golden" eagle over the mantel, even "goldfish" in a bowl (JG, p. 117), it is only incidentally the decor that Clara finds "enlightening" (JG, p. 125). What Clara turns tropistically towards is the "radiant intimacy" of the Denham's domestic relationship.

In the "golden childish worlds" of hymn and fairy tale, Clara "searched in vain" for the "true brittle glitter of duplicity" (JG, p. 38). She does not note the oxymoron, but we do, and we are also invited to wonder whether Clara's "craving for the bizarre and the involved" (JG, p. 101) disposes her to see as gold what, in the Denhams' domestic "radiance" no less than in their drawing room, may be merely gilt.

That there is something wrong with Clara's perception is at least suggested by the frequency with which she is "dazzled." Moreover, she seems to prefer the "confusing blur" and "bright indistinct charm" of her surrogate family to the "bitter illumination" (JG, p. 67) that she is a product of a heredity and an environment she would like to repudiate.

Moving from the first to the second sentence of *Jerusalem the Golden*, we can see how deftly Drabble comments immediately on Clara's aspirations by associating with this dominant light imagery another verbal motif. "She found it hard to trust herself to the mercy of fate, which had managed over the years to convert her greatest shame into one of her greatest assets, and even after years of comparative security she was still prepared for, still half expecting the old gibes to be revived." "Trust", "managed", "convert", "assets", "security", turn the gold of Clara's name into coin. And if, in the second sentence, Clara credits fate with converting the potential liability of her name into an asset, by the second page of the novel she has taken over the transaction as she wonders, "since the reversal of fortune was in fact so complete . . . whether she had not gone so far as deliberately to seek a world in which her name could be a credit and not a shame". Another of her apparent "liabilities other than her name" has been her intelligence, which "had been as a child a source of great trouble to her, for it too had singled her out". This too Clara manages to convert into an asset, when her "shining school reports" (JG, p. 6) win her a state scholarship to the University of London. She had always had "some faint hope that some day it might pay off" and sure enough, the scholarship proves that "somebody somewhere had thought that intelligence was worth paying for". Clara's abilities, like her name, are for her "a means, and not an end, a bargaining power rather than a blessing" (JG, p. 7).

Given this introduction by the narrator, we are not surprised when Clara congratulates herself on her "acquisition" of Clelia Denham (JG, p. 139), takes "on trust" the "new acquisitions"(JG, p. 191) of taste in books, art, and interior decoration she gets from the Denhams, wishes "to set, through [Gabriel], a value on herself" (JG, p. 207), and at last, just before she is finally "able to use his name at last, luxuriously, expensively, across the long distance miles of wires", tells Gabriel, "All you are to me, you know, is a means of self-advancement" (JG, p. 250).

11 Fiona MacCarthy, "The Drabble Sisters", *Guardian* (April 13, 1967), p. 8.
12 Jerome Hamilton Buckley, *Season of Youth: The Bildungsroman from Dickens to Golding* (Cambridge: Harvard University Press, 1974), pp. 17–18.
13 Clara's story diverges from Buckley's paradigm in that she has only one significant love affair, which she sees as exalting rather than debasing (although she admits to Gabriel that "others, I suppose, might see it as a decadence" [JG, p. 250]). And it includes another feature of the genre which Buckley's summary surprisingly omits, the hero's crucial relationship with a mentor, who guides his initiation into the adult world. In the Denhams, Clara finds a whole family of mentors and acknowledges that they serve her in this function:

> She took them on trust so completely, the Denhams, for as far as she could see they were never wrong. And yet trust was not the right word for the way she regarded them, for she did not humbly and ignorantly echo their judgments in her own head; she did not say to herself, repeating what she had heard, I like that advertisement, that house, that film, that book, that painting, that kind of stocking, that man's face. It was rather that she saw what they saw, once they had told her to see it. They taught her, they instructed her . . . (JG, p. 191).

14 Robert Alter, *Rogue's Progress: Studies in the Picaresque Novel* (Cambridge: Harvard University Press, 1964), p. 31.
15 While Clara thinks of her life as a "progress" (JG, pp. 6, 31, 120, 139), Clelia Denham puts into words the question the novel as a whole raises, "whether the alarmingly increased velocity of progress might not perhaps take its toll, some day: whether one person could achieve, in effect, the travelling of many generations" (JG, p. 156). Clara is placed in a fictional context in which true

progress is not measured by velocity but by adaptability and the ability to change as a result of what one learns.

16 She is "drawn unquestionably to the appearance of things", as she herself acknowledges (JG, p. 107); she does not want to know what may lie beneath the surfaces whose glitter dazzles her. When she inadvertently catches a glimpse of real human complexity, she closes her eyes. She wants to believe, for instance, that Gabriel's being married is "merely an added enticement" to having an affair with him, "for she had always fancied the idea of a complicated, illicit and disastrous love" (JG, p. 139). So when she catches a momentary glimpse of the "appalling, exhausting strain" (JG, p. 164) that exists between Gabriel and his wife, that makes their marriage painfully real, she "looked round the room . . . and she drank her whisky very quickly, and did not say no when she was offered some more" (JG, p. 164).

Once she obeys a command to open her eyes. In Paris, at a party, Gabriel's older brother says, "give me a kiss:"

> And she, acquiescent, confused, willing, stood there and shut her eyes and waited, and he said, patiently, "No, no, I said give me a kiss. Open your eyes . . ."
> So she opened her eyes, and saw him, and also the truth of what he had said, which was that she had never kissed a man in her life, she had merely allowed herself to be kissed . . .

For once, Clara tries to change as a result of learning something. She reaches up and kisses Magnus, and the exertion terrifies her:

> She kissed him, on the lips, and she felt that in doing so she was forcing her nature beyond the limits of its spring, that it could not bend back, that it would break rather than bend so far, or bend so far that it would bear the shape of the curve for life. And then she let go of him . . . (JG, p. 225).

So also, as we shall see, does she "let go" of the most important lesson she learns in the whole novel, the lesson of her "true descent".

17 "The girl in *Jerusalem the Golden*", Drabble says, "like Bennett's first hero, is obsessed with escape". As we have seen, she also entertains a "vision of some other world" which expresses itself in light imagery. In this she is also like Richard Larch, who spends his first night in London, walking through the West End, "[drinking] in the mingled glare and glamour of Piccadilly by night, – the remote stars, the high sombre trees, the vast, dazzling interiors of clubs" (Arnold Bennett, *A Man From the North* [1898; rpt. New York: George H. Doran Company, 1911], p. 7). Vertigo, vision, bedazzlement, radiance – these words and variations on them are used throughout *A Man From the North*, as they are in *Jerusalem the Golden*, to describe the young provincial's response to London. It is not only the glitter of London, however, which attracts Richard, but its size: "He rejoiced in London, in its vistas . . ." (MN, p. 58). These vistas are part of the cityscape, but they suggest intellectual and, even more importantly, emotional horizons for Richard too; in London, particularly in the company of the Aked family, Richard frequently has "the disconcerting sensation of emotional horizons suddenly widened" (MN, p. 147). Especially with Adeline

Aked, with whom he imagines he is in love, he has "an intoxicating vision of future felicities" (MN, p. 169).

Similarly, as we have seen, it is not so much London that constitutes a radiant vision for Clara, but the Denham family, Sebastian, Candida, and their exotically named children, Amelia, Magnus, Gabriel, Clelia, and Annunciata. (This is the only one of her novels in which Drabble, who normally chooses plain names like Sarah for her characters, is so fanciful. This may be another, if minor, indebtedness to Bennett, whose heroines bear such names as Carlotta, Leonora, and – in one novel – Annunciata.) Clara's first visit to the Denhams' house is described in language which recalls Richard Larch's sense of bedazzlement. But in fact, Clara's first visit to the Denhams is not modelled on *A Man From the North*, where no similar scene occurs, but on two other Bennett novels. In both *Clayhanger* and *Hilda Lessways*, the protagonists are dazzled, as Clara is, by their first visits to a home very different from their own.

Edwin Clayhanger's response, on his first visit to the Orgreaves' home, anticipates Clara's to the Denhams'. Like her, he initially has "a confused vision" of an interior fuller and more sumptuous than anything he has ever seen:

> Edwin, nervously pulling out his handkerchief and putting it back, had a confused vision of the hall full of little pictures, plates, stools, rugs, and old sword-sheaths. . . . the Orgreave drawing-room had a bay-window and another large window; it was twice as big as the Clayhangers' and of an interesting irregular shape. Although there were in it two unoccupied expanses of carpet, it nevertheless contained what seemed to Edwin immense quantities of furniture of all sorts. Easy-chairs were common, and everywhere. Several bookcases rose to the low ceiling; dozens and dozens of pictures hid the walls; each corner had its little society objects; cushions and candlesticks abounded; the piano was a grand, and Edwin was astounded to see another piano, a small upright, in the further distance; there were even two fireplaces, with two mirrors, two clocks, two sets of ornaments, and two embroidered screens. The general effect was of extraordinary lavish profusion, of wilful, splendid, careless extravagance (Arnold Bennett, *Clayhanger* [1910; rpt. New York: Doubleday, Doran & Company, Inc., 1936], pp. 236–238).

The Denhams' drawing room:

> was a large, high, long room, and so full of furniture and mirrors and pictures and books and chandeliers and hangings and refracted angles of light that the eye could, at first glimpse, in no way assess its dimensions; it was like some infinitely more complicated and elaborate and intentional version of the hall which Clara had first entered. It seemed to be full of alcoves and angles and small grouped areas of being, though the room itself was a plain rectangle. . . . Over the marble mantelpiece was a huge oval gold mirror, with an eagle adorning it, and beneath it two gilt and delicate sprays of candle brackets. The floor was wooden, and polished, but most of it was covered by a large, intricately patterned and badly frayed coloured carpet. On one wall hung a large picture of a classical, mythological nature: on another wall was an equally large picture of undulating pale yellow and

beige lines. The third wall was lined entirely with books, and the wall that looked over the garden was not a wall but a window, heavily shrouded with curtains of different fabrics and densities. Clara was astonished; she could compare the room to nothing in her experience (JG, p. 117).

Clara had been taught in Northam that gilt and tapestry and Persian rugs were vulgar; the unmistakeable authenticity of the Denhams' drawing room "enlightens" her to their true value (JG, p. 125). So Edwin is "enlightened" by the Orgreaves (C, p. 244), who value things his austere father had taught him to scorn, such as music and books and conversation. Both Clara and Edwin remark with wonder that each Denham and Orgreave child has a room of his or her own. Neither can believe the evidence they perceive of affectionate familial relationships. "Edwin . . . thought the relationship between father and sons utterly delightful. He had not conceived that parents and children ever were or could be on such terms" (C, p. 252). Clara "had never in her life seen or heard of such a mother, a mother capable of such pleasant, witty and overt concern, nor had she ever seen such an image of fraternal love" (JG, p. 131). For both Edwin and Clara, the experience is too rich. Edwin leaves the Orgreaves' feeling "intoxicated", not with wine but with "the vision which he had had of the possibilities of being really interested in life" (C, p. 256). By the end of her first evening with the Denhams, Clara's head aches. "Whole concepts, whole reorganizations of thought swam drunkenly through her head . . . when she got home she was suddenly and violently sick. She could not assimilate, however hard she willed to do so, such strange food" (JG, p. 129).

[18] Cynthia Griffin Wolff, *A Feast of Words: The Triumph of Edith Wharton* (New York: Oxford University Press, 1977), p. 92.

[19] Ibid.

[20] Arnold Bennett, *Hilda Lessways* (1911; rpt. New York: Doubleday, Doran & Company, Inc., 1936), p. 137. Further references to HL will appear in the text.

[21] Margaret Drabble, "The Fearful Fame of Arnold Bennett", *Observer* (May 11, 1967), pp. 12–14.

[22] Bergonzi, op. cit.

[23] Leon Edel, *Literary Biography* (1959; rpt. Bloomington: Indiana University Press, 1973), p. 10.

[24] Roger Sale, "Huxley and Bennett, Bedford and Drabble", *Hudson Review*, Vol. XXVIII, No. 2 (Summer 1975), 289.

[25] "The Fearful Fame of Arnold Bennett".

[26] Margaret Drabble, "The Author Comments" on Monica Lauritzen Mannheimer, "The Search for Identity in Margaret Drabble's *The Needle's Eye*", *Dutch Quarterly Review of Anglo-American Letters*, Vol. 5, No. 1 (1975), 35–38.

3 "The most female of all my books": *The Waterfall*

In *A Summer Bird-Cage, The Garrick Year*, and *The Millstone*, as in *The Second Sex*, the question of autonomy is linked to matters of sex and of gender. All three of Drabble's early heroines have trouble with sex because they believe that yielding to its "impersonal pulls" will condemn them to what de Beauvoir calls "immanence" ("confinement or restriction to a narrow round of uncreative and repetitious duties . . . in contrast to the freedom to engage in projects of ever widening scope that marks the untrammelled existent", TSS, p. 58) and Sarah Bennett more simply calls "kitchens and gas-meters and draughts under the door and tiresome quarrels". At the same time, they sense that their very identity as women is profoundly connected with their sexuality. In *The Second Sex*, de Beauvoir asks whether it is possible to be a woman and an autonomous and transcendent subject, thus engaging the problematic situation of women in all its complexity. By 1966, Margaret Drabble seems to have realized that it was too complex for her. So in *Jerusalem the Golden* she lays aside questions of sex and gender to deal with what must have seemed to her a more fundamental question: is it possible or desirable to be autonomous and transcendent?

For although its protagonist is a woman, *Jerusalem the Golden* is not a "women's novel". Unlike Drabble's earlier heroines, Clara Maugham is neither threatened nor trammelled by her sex; she is afforded the same opportunities for self-realization that patriarchy has traditionally offered intelligent young men, and she exploits them as ruthlessly as Julien Sorel. Moreover, Drabble not only creates a heroine whose situation is not explained by her sex, she writes her history according to a generic model which is, if not male, then certainly neuter. *Jerusalem the Golden* is not a "female *Bildungsroman*";[1] it is simply a *Bildungsroman*.

49

On the other hand, Drabble has called *The Waterfall* "the most female of all my books".[2] With a new awareness of what autonomy might mean, Drabble again asks the Beauvoirian question that generated her first novel, "is it possible to be a woman and an autonomous and transcendent subject?" Her answer is more optimistic than de Beauvoir's.

At the heart of de Beauvoir's feminism, as Patricia Meyer Spacks has noted, is her insistence that "the notion of 'femininity' is a fiction created by men," who tell woman "that passivity and acceptance are her nature".[3] De Beauvoir accuses men of condemning women to the condition she calls "alterity":

> Now, what peculiarly signalizes the situation of woman is that she – a free and autonomous being like all human creatures – nevertheless finds herself living in a world where men compel her to assume the status of the Other. They propose to stabilize her as object and to doom her to immanence (TSS, p. xxviii).

Implicit in de Beauvoir's analysis of the situation of woman is the idea that patriarchy has projected the conflict between an individual's animal and rational natures onto a conflict between the sexes, in which man is defined as rational and woman as animal:

> Just as for the ancients there was an absolute vertical with reference to which the oblique was defined, so there is an absolute human type, the masculine. . . . Thus humanity is male and man defines woman not in herself but as relative to him. . . . she appears essentially to the male as a sexual being. For him she is sex – absolute sex, no less (TSS, pp. xv-xvi).

But *The Second Sex* is more than a feminist's description of the situation of women. It is also an attempt to understand why "this has always been a man's world". De Beauvoir finds the answer by "reviewing the data of prehistoric research and ethnography in the light of existentialist philosophy." (TSS, p. 56). And her existentialist analysis is at odds with her feminist contention that "one is not born, but rather becomes, a woman", as Jean Leighton, her acute if sympathetic critic, has so clearly shown. When she turns her attention from the "situation" of woman to her ontological status, de Beauvoir finds that what dooms her to immanence is not men but biology.

"Not only has man decided what are the values of the tribe and imposed them upon his 'inferior half' ", but from an existentialist perspective, "man's original functions have been in fact intrinsically superior to woman's".[4] Although the feminist de Beauvoir asserts that "no biological, psychological, or economic fate determines the figure that the human female presents in society" (TSS, p. 249), the existentialist in her sees woman's biology as absolutely determinant:

> The woman who gave birth, therefore, did not know the pride of creation; she felt herself the plaything of obscure forces, and the painful ordeal of childbirth seemed a useless or even troublesome accident. But in any case giving birth and suckling are not activities, they are natural functions; no project is involved . . . (TSS, p. 57).

Woman's biological role as child-bearer "imprison[s] her in repetition and immanence" (TSS, pp. 57–58). Man, on the other hand, transcends his "animal nature" through activity, through projects by which he "remodels the face of the earth, he creates new instruments, he invents, he shapes the future" (TSS, p. 59). For the existentialist de Beauvoir, "man's power and transcendence make him fully 'existent' while woman, doomed to immanence and passivity, is not really 'existent' or even as fully human as the male".[5] Thus de Beauvoir's existentialism not only accepts the patriarchal distinction between spirit (transcendence) and flesh (immanence), but endorses the patriarchal projection of that distinction onto the sexes. All individuals, in order to become "existents", must transcend the flesh, but some – namely women – may not be able to. In de Beauvoir's philosophy, if not in her feminism, "woman's immanence, passivity, and essential entrapment by her biological destiny are the initial sources of her malediction".[6] For Simone de Beauvoir, as for men, "woman is always 'the other' ".[7]

Not as a philosopher, but as an imaginative writer and as a woman, Drabble attacks this proposition in *The Waterfall*. By 1969, she may have perceived that in exhorting women to transcend the definition men have assigned them as the Other, the sex, de Beauvoir is covertly exhorting them to deny their sexuality. Even in her first novel, whose heroine has internalized the patriarchal dichotomies between spirit and flesh, immanence and transcendence, being a woman and being a fully existent human being,

Drabble voices her suspicion of these antitheses. While she would certainly agree with de Beauvoir that woman is not *the* Other, she insists that she contains within herself *an* Other, the "pulls of sex and blood" which "drag [Sarah Bennett] into unwilled motion" and cause her to reject the "sexless" Simone as a model.

The Second Sex, Jean Leighton writes, "staunchly insists" that "action and transcendence are male and good; being and immanence are feminine and bad".[8] *Jerusalem the Golden*, with its "masculine" heroine, challenges the premise that action and "transcendence" are good; *The Waterfall* begins by accepting the premise that immanence and passivity are feminine. It is "the most female of all [Drabble's] books" not because, as she suggests, it begins with childbirth and ends with a thrombic-clot induced by contraceptive pill-taking,[9] but because it considers the situation of a woman who does not deny her femininity, whose first words in the novel, far from asserting her will, announce her essential passivity: "If I were drowning I couldn't reach a hand to save myself, so unwilling am I to set myself up against my fate".[10]

Fate is a word and a concept which pervades Margaret Drabble's fiction. In *The Millstone* it took on vaguely Freudian, or at least deterministic, overtones, as Rosamund sought to explain and excuse her frigidity in terms of her early childhood experiences. In *Jerusalem the Golden*, it is the burden of heredity which Clara would wrongly like to shrug off. In *The Waterfall*, it becomes more complex and closer to the thematic core of the novel, but at least on one level it is gender. For Jane Gray, as for Freud, "anatomy is destiny".

Jane's ideas about fate should be distinguished from Drabble's, who reflected in her interview with Nancy Hardin that she's "kind of Greek with a Greek view of the gods". When Jane thinks of Oedipus and fate, however, she is recalling not Sophocles but Seneca who, as Moses Hadas points out, "is concerned not to justify the ways of gods to men or of men to gods, but to display the capacity for emotional intensity exhibited by characters endowed with extraordinary passions".[11] When Jane ventures to think about the ways of gods to men, she quickly becomes personal:

> What right had any deity to submit mortality to such obsessive, arbitrary powers? The meaningless violence of the world – the Lisbon earthquake, the *Titanic*, Aberfan – has given thought to better minds than mine, but at least these disasters are external, and can be ascribed to a hostile, ill-ordered universe: not so the

violence of our own bodies, as unwilled, as foreordained, as the sliding of mountains, the uprooting of trees, the tidal waves of the sea (W, p. 182).

The "fate" that Jane acknowledges has its seat in her "guts" and she claims to be powerless to resist it. "I do not accuse myself of weakness of will. There had been nothing else to do. There had never been a question of choice. There had been nothing in me capable of choosing. I had done what I had to do, I had done what my nature was . . ." (W, p. 183). What my *feminine* nature was, she should have said. For as Drabble's language makes clear, Jane is governed by her female sexuality.

"So liquid we are, inside our stiff bodies", Jane reflects (W, p. 229). Emma Evans would have agreed, but she would have wanted to ignore it. Don't go near the water, she warns her daughter. Don't get wet "with milk and blood and tears, a varied sea of grief". *The Waterfall* is a revision of the understory of *The Garrick Year*, not of the events which comprise the narrative action but of the psychic and symbolic events which underscore its essential theme, the problem of female sexuality.

Emma Evans, as we have seen, fears death by drowning. She weans her child as soon as she can and tries to ignore the tuggings of her guts. Through all sorts of symbolic acts, she seeks to deny her essentially *liquid* female identity. Jane Gray, on the other hand, enjoys the warm dampness of the room in which, as the novel begins, she gives birth to her second child. She lets her sweat and her blood flow without embarrassment or distaste and likes the "thin warm wetness" of the tea the midwife gives her because "it was liquid and warm, like weeping. . . . Jane let her whole body weep and flow, graciously, silently submitting herself to these cruel events, to this pain, to this deliverance" (W, p. 7). Deliverance. Not the usual word for giving birth, which is "delivery". Deliverance connotes setting free, rescue, release from bondage, and it is the word Jane applies to the act James, her cousin's husband, performs for her in making love to her and thus awakening and releasing her sexual, womanly self.

Jane's situation at the beginning of *The Waterfall* resembles Emma's at the conclusion of *The Garrick Year*. Although married and a mother, she has withheld herself from her husband and her child, maintaining what she calls her "dry integrity" (W, p. 181) as a poet and a purely private individual. She is also, like Emma

Evans, neurotic. When her husband, less tolerant of her "bad housekeeping" and "too evident frigidity" (W, p. 130) than David Evans had been of Emma's, leaves her in the seventh month of her second pregnancy, Jane retreats into total isolation. Her first child is staying with his grandparents, so she has no reason to leave her house, and doesn't. "She did not ring her parents to tell them that her husband had left her, because she preferred to be alone. She wandered round the cold and empty house, watching the rain fall outside, seeing the windows silt up with London grime, watching the dust thicken on the furniture. She did nothing". She doesn't even bother to heat her meals: "she ate baked beans and sardines and asparagus straight from the tins". Indeed, "the temperature of her life seemed to be cooling into some ice age of inactivity" (W, p. 4).

And then her labour begins and although "she could hardly bring herself to summon the midwife, so reluctant was she to see and to be seen," she does, and delivers her child in a room made warm and damp by the electric heaters the midwife has brought in from other rooms. Lying on her bed, which is "warm and sodden" with the blood and sweat of her giving birth, Jane feels not only peace, but a sense of expectancy: "Deliverance seemed at hand. It would be safe to wait, now: it could no longer be missed or avoided. This close heat would surely generate its own salvation" (W, p. 7). What the heat generates is Jane's sexual awakening. Her cousin Lucy, with her husband James, comes to relieve the midwife and sit with Jane and her new daughter. After the first few days, Lucy returns to her own house and children, leaving James to spend his nights in the house with Jane. Jane responds with passive enjoyment to his commands that she eat or drink or go to sleep: "Looking back, she was amazed at the ease with which she had drifted away; there was a sense in which she had taken his words as an order and had, unprotesting, obeyed" (W, p. 36). And when he tells her he loves her, "she flinched and sighed, alarmed and yet hopelessly moved by his willing blind suicidal dive into such deep waters; the waters closed over their heads, and they lay there, submerged, the cold dry land of non-loving abandoned" (W, p. 40).

Jane begins "to live for his coming, submitting herself helplessly to the current" (W, p. 42) of his passion for her, and when the necessary six weeks of post-partum healing are over, they make love. The previously frigid Jane is "astonished . . . that a desire so primitive could flow through her":

And so they fell asleep, damp, soaked in a mutual flood of emotion, hardly covered by the stained and wrinkled sheet. One of the things she had always most feared in love had been the wetness. It had dismayed and haunted her, that fatal moisture, and she had surrounded herself with towels and tissues, arid, frightened, fighting like a child for the cold flat dry confines of a narrow bed, superstitiously afraid, like a child, of the body's warmth: and now she lay there, drowned in a willing sea (W, p. 51).

Soon after their first sexual encounter, Jane experiences her first orgasm:

[James] had taken her too far, and she would never get back to the dry integrity she had once inhabited . . . she could not move but had to lie there, tense, breaking, afraid, the tears unshed standing up in the rims of her eyes, her body about to break apart with the terror of being left alone right up there on that high dark painful shelf, with everything falling away dark on all sides of her, alone and high up, stranded, unable to fall. Then suddenly but slowly for the first time ever, just as she thought she must die without him forever, she started to fall, painfully, anguished, but falling at last, falling, coming toward him, meeting him at last, down there in his arms, half dead but not dead, crying out to him, trembling, shuddering, quaking, drenched and drowned, down there at last in the water, not high in her lonely place . . . (W, pp. 181–181)

And James? "He wanted her, he too had sweated for this deliverance". He is rewarded by her inarticulate cries of pleasure: "Her own voice, in that strange sobbing cry of rebirth. A woman delivered" (W, p. 181).

In a sense Jane Gray is Emma Evans' daughter. Ignoring her mother's warning, she gets wet with "milk and blood and tears" and is thus ready for her sexual initiation, her release into total fulfillment as a woman.

Understandably, some feminist critics have a hard time with *The Waterfall*. They see Jane not as delivered from arid neurosis but as delivered into sexual bondage.[12] Jane herself contemplates "the extent of [her] subjugation" to James: "I even went so far as to look it up in a sexual textbook – an old-fashioned one, Havelock Ellis, I think – where I found the word 'bondage,' which seemed quite

elegantly to describe my condition. I was in bondage" (W, p. 183).
But Jane is aware, as her critics are not, that this bondage
paradoxically liberates her:

> It is a fact that I lived alone and lay there alone, that I spoke to no
> one, that I was unable to confront the sight of a human face. It is a
> fact that I regarded James as a miracle, and that when he touched
> me it was as though I had another body, a body different from the
> one I had known. Perhaps I had always possessed it: but without
> him, where would it have lived? What shadowy realms would it
> have inhabited? A body must take on flesh for us to know it. And
> without James, where would it have been, where would I have
> been, where would have lived the woman that writes these words?
> He changed me, he saved me, he changed me. I say it again, there
> is nothing else to say. It is too much to lay at his charge, but it was
> he that did it: but for him, where would I now have been? Alone
> and mad, perhaps . . . (W, p. 277).

Emma Evans, as we have seen, is divided, split between her
"self", characterized by intelligence and will, and her body, "the
part of me that was not me, but just any old thing, the inside of me,
the blood and muscle and water and skin and bone of me, the
rubbish". Similarly, Jane Gray feels "split . . . or perhaps less split
than divided". But unlike Emma, Jane feels "a possibility of
reconciliation":

> My mind did not reject my body, nor my body my mind, and
> indeed these two words ill describe the states or levels on which I
> lived, for the bodily level was in many ways more profound, more
> human, more myself. . . . And in my second childbirth, as I bore
> Bianca, I think I could feel . . . that I was coming together
> again, that I could no longer support the division, that my flesh
> and mind must meet or die (W, p. 123).

Jane finds reconciliation in *willing* her own subjugation to James
and the flesh. If anatomy is destiny, then – so *The Waterfall* would
seem to be saying – "one is not released from the fated pattern, one
must walk it till death." But "sometimes," as in the case of Jane
Gray, "one may find a way of walking that pre-destined path more
willingly" (W, p. 194).

It might be argued, of course, that this is not so much

reconciliation as capitulation, that in willing her subjugation, Jane Gray is defining herself wholly as "the Other", "the sex". But it is important to examine Jane's statement of what James has done for her. He has put her in touch not only with her body, but with her *voice*. "A body must take on flesh for us to know it. And without James, where would it have been, where would I have been, where would have lived the woman that writes these words?" "I" here is an amalgam of the flesh and the word, the animal *and* the rational.

Perhaps the most obvious formal feature of *The Waterfall* is the split in its narrative structure. The first sentence of the novel suggests that it will be narrated in the first person: "If I were drowning I couldn't reach out a hand to save myself, so unwilling am I to set myself up against my fate". Reading on, however, one discovers that this opening sentence must be read as a direct quotation from a protagonist named first "she", then "Jane", and finally, on page 15, "Mrs. Gray". The first fifty pages of the novel are a dramatic narration of Jane's confinement and delivery and of the growth and consummation of her passion for James. It has the shape and unity of a dramatic act or scene, and it ends with a peroration I have already quoted:

> And so they fell asleep, damp, soaked in a mutual flood of emotion, hardly covered by the stained and wrinkled sheet. One of the things she had always most feared in love had been the wetness. It had dismayed and haunted her, that fatal moisture, and she had surrounded herself with towels and tissues, arid, frightened, fighting like a child for the cold flat dry confines of a narrow bed, superstitiously afraid, like a child, of the body's warmth: and now she lay there, drowned in a willing sea.

There follows a white space. When the next section of the novel begins, the reader is immediately disconcerted, for it is narrated in the first person: "It won't, of course, do: as an account, I mean, of what took place". The rest of *The Waterfall* alternates between sections of first- and third-person narration, some of them long enough to beguile the reader into believing she or he is reading a conventional, straightforward novel in either the first- or third-person narrational mode. Then, when the reader's guard is lowered, the narrative mode shifts. The effect continues to be startling.

When Peter Firchow interviewed Drabble, he mentioned this aspect of *The Waterfall* and asked whether she, hitherto a realist in the Arnold Bennett tradition, might be moving "toward more experimental kinds of writing". Drabble firmly denied that this had been her intention. *The Waterfall*, she said, "wasn't experimental in the sense that one didn't know what was going on":

> I hate books which are deliberately confusing. I aim to be lucid. If one doesn't know what one's writing, I don't see why one should write it. . . . I wrote the first chunk [of *The Waterfall*] in the third person and found it impossible to continue with, because it did not seem to me to tell anything like the whole story. And so I evolved. I didn't intend when I started the book to have this shifting, but it did seem quite a useful device, having got it set up. But it wasn't my aim at all to write it experimentally.

This statement by Drabble is entirely consistent with her frequently recorded preference for the traditional novel. Why then did it feel right to her to fiddle with narrative voice in *The Waterfall*?

One possible answer is suggested by her saying to Firchow that it was impossible to tell "anything like the whole story" in the third person. If Jane Gray's is the whole story of what it means to be female, and if being female means feeling divided, then it would certainly be appropriate, if not necessary, to depict that division formally. But the first- and third-person narrators do not neatly correspond to the division Jane Gray experiences, between what she calls "flesh and mind".

That is because the whole story of *The Waterfall* is not simply what it means to be female. What it *is* is suggested by Drabble's confession to Firchow that there was at least one "experimental novelist" she admired: "My favourite experimental novelist is Doris Lessing – *The Golden Notebook*, actually". *The Golden Notebook* is about a protagonist who is a woman and a novelist. As a woman she feels, like Jane Gray, divided – her word is "fragmented". This sense of inner division affects her ability to write; she fragments her experience into various notebooks and projects aspects of herself and her experience onto several fictional alter-egos in the novels she is attempting to write. *The Golden Notebook* is a great novel, comprehending much more than the experience of being a woman. It is also about political consciousness and responsibility, history, and perhaps most insistently about the relationship between art and life. Although *The Waterfall* is in every way a smaller book than *The*

Golden Notebook, I believe Drabble was right when she told Firchow that Lessing's novel had "profoundly affected" her.

The whole story of *The Waterfall* is the same as one of the stories *The Golden Notebook* tells, what it means not only to be a woman but to be a woman writer. Thus it is not only the most female of Drabble's novels, but may be the most personal as well, just as *The Golden Notebook* is the most personal of Lessing's novels. The difference between the two novels is that Lessing knew perfectly well what she was doing, while Drabble seems to have been unaware of the metafictional status of *The Waterfall* and of its relevance to her situation as a woman novelist.

Lessing's Anna Wulf is a novelist, quite possibly a surrogate for the novelist Doris Lessing. Certainly her writer's block, which Lessing says in her 1971 preface to *The Golden Notebook* was central to her conception of Anna Wolf's character, is caused by the same disparity between life and art Lessing herself feels so strongly. So too, although Drabble does not encourage us to make the association, can Jane Gray be seen as a surrogate for the novelist Margaret Drabble.

Jane Gray is a poet. She is also, by virtue of the "experimental" form of *The Waterfall*, a novelist. For as the first-person sections of the novel reveal, Jane is writing about her experience with James, and writing as novelist, with a concern for such things as "style", "medium", "narrative", "sequence", and "form". She is even aware of how she paragraphs her account of her love affair with James (W, p. 156). On page 275, Jane Gray claims authorship for *The Waterfall* (as Anna Wulf is revealed as the author of the novel-within-a-novel in *The Golden Notebook*, the five-sectioned "Free Women"): "At the beginning of this book, I deliberately exaggerated my helplessness . . ."

I believe that Margaret Drabble devised the odd, if not exactly experimental, form of *The Waterfall* to tell "the whole story," the story first – as I have indicated – of what it means to be a woman, and second of what it means to be a woman novelist. What Drabble has done, intuitively it seems, is to find a form that expresses not only the divisions within the woman but within the artist who is also a woman.

It is not until page 52 that the reader realizes that *The Waterfall* is the depiction of this second divided self. For there, abruptly, after fifty pages of third-person narration, Jane Gray reveals that she has been telling her own story and that "it", the third-person narration, "won't, of course, do: as an account, I mean, of what took place".

Why won't it do? Because Jane hasn't "told the truth, about myself and James" (W, p. 52). She has not lied, she has "omitted: merely, professionally, edited". Because she sees "true virtue in clarity, in consistency", she has "omitted everything" from her account of their coming together in that birthing room "except that sequence of discovery and recognition that I would call love" (W, p. 52). She has, to borrow terminology from E. M. Forster's *Aspects of the Novel*, transformed story into plot, "in terms of narrative and consequence" (W, p. 55). Incapable of "enduring" the "one event" that comprises her recent history (W, p. 52), she subjects it to the scrutinizing analysis of art:

> I must make an effort to comprehend it. I will take it all to pieces, I will resolve it to its parts, and then I will put it together again, I will reconstitute it in a form that I can accept, a fictitious form: adding a little here, abstracting a little there, moving this arm half an inch that way, gently altering the dead angle of the head upon its neck (W, p. 59).

Returning to the first long section of *The Waterfall*, the reader will see signs of Jane's artistic reconstitution of what must have been the actual sequence of thought and enacted events. The first sentence of the "novel" written by Jane Gray begins with drowning:

> If I were drowning I couldn't reach out a hand to save myself, so unwilling am I to set myself up against my fate. This is what she said to [Malcolm, her husband] one night. He was not interested, and she had not expected him to be so. She had not even thought, as she said it, that it might be the truth. But the image, nevertheless, remained with her, as though she had by accident articulated something of significance.

Whether or not Jane ever said that first sentence to her husband is less important than the use Jane Gray makes of the image of drowning in her fictional account of how she came to fall in love with James Otford. The first section of Jane Gray's novel ends, as it began with this image: "she lay there [in the bed with James], drowned in a willing sea". And between the first and last sentences of this first section of the novel, Jane Gray describes her heroine in watery terms.

Of course I have pointed out this pattern of imagery before, but it is important to note that it is an image chosen and developed by Jane Gray the artist, in an effort to shape and explain the experience she has had as a woman. In *Thinking About Women*, Mary Ellmann recalls Freud's association of solidity (form) with maleness, liquidity (formlessness) with femaleness, and reflects that, in Western literature, "solid ground is masculine, the sea is feminine".[13] Extending this distinction further, we might reflect that in Western literature, reality is feminine and art is masculine; what is formless is given form. Jane Gray is working in this tradition.[14] She has divided herself into Jane, the woman (whose experience is liquid and formless), and Jane Gray, the artist (who gives form, order, and shapeliness to that experience).

But although Jane Gray is an artist, she is also a woman, and the essentially male form of her art does not express her "actual apprehension of what it is like to be a woman, the irreconcilable difference of it – that sense of living one's deepest life under water . . ."[15] And in the first person, she acknowledges that her shapely fiction about Jane is nothing but "lies, lies, it's all lies". "What have I tried to describe? A passion, a love, an unreal life, a life in limbo, without anxiety, guilt, corpses; no albatross, no sin, no weariness, no aching swollen untouchable breasts, no bleeding womb, but the pure flower of love itself . . ." (W, p. 98). The drama of *The Waterfall* consists in the reconciliation of Jane Gray's divided self, the coming together of the woman who experiences love as "a quotidian reality" (W, p. 99) and the artist who shapes that experience into "a fictitious passion" (W, p. 243). In this drama, Jane Gray plays two roles: woman and the woman artist. And in the second of these she is a surrogate for Margaret Drabble, whose struggle in *The Waterfall* may be understood in terms of Elaine Showalter's distinction between "books that happen to have been written by women" and "a female literature . . . which purposefully and collectively concerns itself with the articulation of women's experience, and which guides itself by its own impulses to autonomous self-expression".[16]

Jane's task as woman and as artist is the same: to acknowledge the existence within her self of the Other and not simply to reconcile but to encompass that division. As a woman, she does this by discovering, with James, her essentially passive sexuality and then refusing to be defined solely in terms of it. For it is important to see that Jane does not remain in sexual bondage to James, that by the end of the novel she has reasserted the rational, productive, "masculine" aspect of her self (she cleans up her house, hires an *au pair* girl, writes and has published "a very good sequence of poems" [W, p. 283]), while at the same time keeping in touch with the passive, sexual, "feminine" self that James has aroused. As an artist, Jane Gray must find a way of incorporating into her shapely, Apollonian, "male" fiction some of the inchoate, liquid "femininity" of her experience. The form of Drabble's fiction, with its alternation of first- and third-person sections, enables her to show the merger of these two aspects of Jane Gray. Initially there is a clear division between the "I" who meditates on the art of writing and the "she" who has a love affair with James Otford. But toward the end of the novel, these distinctions blur. Metafictional meditations occur at least once in the third-person sections (see pp. 242–250, for an example) and the first-person sections become "agonized", as "I" claims and acknowledges as her own the experiences of "her". Finally, on page 274, "I" and "she" come together, as a section which begins in the third-person switches to the first. This signals the unification of the divided self who is Jane Gray.

The process by which this unification is achieved may be observed by looking closely, in sequence, at the first-person sections of *The Waterfall*. In the first of these, which begins after the first section of what I have called Jane Gray's novel about Jane, Jane Gray reveals herself as an Apollonian artist, seeking to shape and edit her experience into form and thus give it meaning. But already, there are signs that she is dissatisfied with her art. "I flinched at the conclusion", she says, at the shapely conclusion of the first chapter, in which Jane lies "drowned in a willing sea" of passion with James. "I" in this sentence is not "I, the artist" but "I, the whole (female) person" who sees in her "hesitance" at writing that conclusion a "virtue", even though it is "inartistic". Art demands closure, "conclusions". But in making conclusions about what is, in fact, inconclusive, fiction may be telling lies.

At this early stage in *The Waterfall*, however, Jane Gray seldom feels hesitant about giving form to her experience. Indeed, she seems to believe that it has intrinsic form, that her affair with James was ordained by destiny: "Grace and miracles. I don't much care for my terminology. Though at least it lacks that most disastrous concept, the concept of free will. . . . Necessity is my God. Necessity lay with me when James did" (W, p. 56).

But her doubts persist and indeed become insistent. In her next meditation on the art of fiction, Jane Gray acknowledges that she has supplied plot, a sequence of cause and effect, to her remembered affair, thus creating "the narrative tale, the narrative explanation" (W, p. 77) which is not completely true to life. Unwilling yet to confront reality, Jane Gray decides to "go back to that other story, to that other woman, who lived a life too pure, too lovely to be mine" (W, p. 78).

In the next first-person section, however, Jane calls her novel "a pack of lies" and resolves to make "some effort to comprehend" what she has excluded from it (W, pp. 98–99). There follow, in the first-person, a long account of Jane's relationship with her husband Malcolm and an attempt to review her story "from the point of view of Lucy" (W, p. 135). It is during this long passage of first-person narration that Jane Gray reveals that she stopped writing poetry when she began her affair with James. She senses, and we see quite clearly, that it is because her poetry will not accommodate her female experience; her verse is "flawlessly metrical, and it always rhymed" (W, p. 129); she can "find no words or patterns for the damp and intimate secrets of love" (W, p. 130). In her "novel", as in her poetry, Jane Gray must discover these words.

The effort of looking at her experience whole and trying to comprehend it proves, at this point, too much for Jane Gray. "I am getting tired of all this Freudian family nexus, I want to get back to that schizoid third-person dialogue. I've got one or two more sordid conditions to describe, and then I can get back there to that isolated world of pure corrupted love" (W, p. 155). "I'm tired of all this", she says. "It has a certain kind of truth, but it isn't the truth I care for" (W, p. 156).

The turning point in Jane Gray's slow but gradual progress to becoming a woman writer comes not in one of the first-person sections of *The Waterfall* but in one of the chapters of Jane Gray's novel, as if she were able to articulate only through her fictional alter-ego a negative judgment about the kind of poetry (and fiction) she writes. James has just performed a stunning trick with playing cards, which Jane admires – with important reservations:

"I think it's the symmetry I like", she said, gazing at the new card pattern that he had just nonchalantly created. "I find it – significant. But I don't know why. It's like rhyme in verse. It's no good, you know, rhymes in verse are a trivial matter, as trivial as playing cards, as pointless as fast cars. It's no good, any of it. It doesn't do any good. I try to justify it, I try so hard, but there isn't any justification, there isn't any meaning. It can't be important, poetry" (W, p. 177).

That, of course, is an extreme statement, an exaggeration, one which will clearly not be wholly acceptable to the artist, Jane Gray. But it is one way of saying that a certain kind of poetry (rhymed and flawlessly metrical) and a certain kind of fiction (shaped, plotted, "closed") do not adequately represent Jane Gray's female experience.

It is, at any rate, after this criticism of poetry that "I" takes over the account of the love affair, or at least shares it with "her". And the "I" who had wanted to see her love affair as fated, shaped by destiny, begins to acknowledge the random, the haphazard, the chancey. She and James have a car accident which is "so horrific in its ghastly disproportion between cause and effect" (W, p. 222) that it "dreadfully" reinforces Jane Gray's "views of providence, of Divine Providence, of the futility of human effort against the power that holds us" (W, pp. 222–223). In this mood, she is surprised and somewhat dismayed to discover that James is not dead: "It would have been so much simpler if he had been dead: so natural a conclusion, so poetic in its justice" (W, p. 228). Jane Gray is still confused, at least in her terminology. Because poetic justice, as she must still learn, is not "natural" at all.

In her final meditation on the art of fiction, Jane Gray reviews her enterprise and tests it against reality. "I was hoping", she says, "that in the end I would manage to find some kind of unity" (W, p. 250). Instead she, who as an artist has maintained that her characters "were predetermined, unalterable, helpless in the hands of destiny" (W, p. 276), discovers that it is "foolish to deny the accidental" (W, p. 277). The car accident, which she says "had given shape and form to my guilt" (W, p. 236), has deprived her fiction of *its* shape and form. According to the rules of fiction, James should have died, "as all true fictional lovers die" (W, p. 236). But he doesn't, and therefore "there isn't any conclusion" to Jane Gray's novel:

A death would have been the answer, but nobody died. Perhaps I should have killed James in the car, and that would have made a neat, a possible ending.
    A feminine ending?
    Or I could have maimed James so badly, in this narrative, that

I would have been allowed to have him, as Jane Eyre had her blinded Rochester. But I hadn't the heart to do it, I loved him too much, and anyway it wouldn't have been the truth because the truth is that he recovered (W, p. 280).

It would not have been a feminine, but a masculine ending to Jane Gray's novel to kill or maim James. A feminine ending, as the poet Jane Gray should know, is inconclusive and undramatic; it is "an unstressed syllable at the end of an iambic or an anapestic line, which would not ordinarily have such a syllable".[17]

"We should have died, I suppose, James and I. It isn't artistic to linger on like this", Jane muses. More accurately, she might have reflected that lingering on frustrates the impulse to closure which characterizes our literary tradition, which is predominantly male. Jane Gray searches "for a conclusion, for an elegant vague figure that would wipe out all the conflict, all the bitterness, all the compromise that is yet to be endured" (W, p. 280), but the best she can come up with is a "finale" which is both "gratuitous" and "irrelevant" (W, p. 286), an account of a trip she and James made in the summer after the accident to Goredale Scar, which unlike Jane Gray's fictional representation of Jane's and James's love, is a "real . . . example of the sublime" (W, p. 286).What encourages us to think that Jane Gray may be discovering what it means to be a woman artist is her discovery that the sublime is followed by the ridiculous. The Goredale Scar is "a lovely organic balance of shapes and curves" (W, p. 287) like a perfect poem, but Jane Gray does not "conclude" her story there. Instead she recounts what happened when she and James returned to their hotel room:

I poured myself a glassful [of whiskey] . . . and went to have a bath, to wash off the mud. When I came back and got into bed I must have left my glass on James's side of the bed because much later in the night he took a mouthful of the unfinished drink, and spat it out again violently, saying that it tasted unbelievably foul. I protested, and tasted it myself, but he was right: it tasted dreadful, ancient, musty, of dust and death, and when we put the light on to examine it we saw that I had spilled talcum powder into it, that the Scotch was covered with a thin white chalky film. Scotch and dust. A fitting conclusion to the sublimities of nature (W, p. 289).

But even an ironic conclusion is too conclusive, so Jane Gray appends a one-page "postscript" to her novel:

> No, I can't leave it without a postscript, without formulating that final, indelicate irony. I had at one point thought of the idea of ending the narrative not so much with James's death as with his impotence: the little, twentieth-century death. (I feel ashamed, now, to have had so vicious a notion.) But in fact the truth is quite otherwise, for if we hadn't had that accident, I would quite possibly have died myself of thrombosis: since Bianca's birth I had been taking the relevant pills and would probably have gone on taking them until they killed me, which they might have well done, preferring the present to the future, however dangerously. I think I mentioned that on the eve of our departure to Norway I lay awake imagining a pain in my leg: well, it was a real pain, it was a swelling, a thrombic clot. The price that modern woman must pay for love. In the past, in old novels, the price of love was death, a price which virtuous women paid in childbirth, and the wicked, like Nana, with the pox. Nowadays it is paid in thrombosis or neurosis: one can take one's pick. I stopped taking those pills, as James lay there unconscious and motionless, but one does not escape decision so easily. I am glad of this. I am glad I cannot swallow pills with immunity. I prefer to suffer, I think (W, p. 290).

This postscript is a triumph of feminine form. Not only does its "indelicate irony" undercut the purely fictional sublimity of Jane's affair with James, but it successfully resists its own impulse to make a final formulation. The last dramatic, heroic, "masculine" statement – "I prefer to suffer" – is followed by the feminine ending, "I think".

2

In December of 1975, at the annual convention of the Modern Language Association, a panel of women discussed the question of whether women novelists constituted a distinct group. They asked not only whether women writers possessed a distinct subject matter (whether they did or should write "about" women), but whether they also had a unique task (to write "for" women). Nancy Milford admitted, somewhat apologetically, that she read books by women novelists as if they were "guide-books",[18] and most of the panelists agreed that the woman novelist has an essentially heuristic obligation. She can "illuminate" women's experience; more importantly she should present models that "affirm" women's potential for self-realization.

On several occasions, Margaret Drabble has endorsed this view of the woman novelist's function. Like Nancy Milford, she has said that she "can't read quietly or objectively", that when she reads novels she's looking "for guidance or help or illumination of some sort or another".[19] Reviewing Doris Lessing's *Stories* for the *Saturday Review*, she observed that "Doris Lessing makes the point that most of us read books with this question in our mind: What does this say about my life?" and quoted the heroine of *The Golden Notebook*, who says "We have to believe in our own beautiful, impossible blueprints".[20] Earlier, in an interview with Lessing published in *Ramparts*, Drabble had quoted the same line, appropriating it for her own definition of the function of the novel: "in writing novels we create not only a book but a future, we draw up through our characters 'our beautiful, impossible blueprints,' and bring into being what we need to be".[21] Her most explicit and extended exposition of this idea occurs in an article entitled simply "A Woman Writer":

> Many people read novels in order to find patterns or images for a possible future – to know how to behave, what to hope to be like. We do not want to resemble the women of the past, but where is our future? This is precisely the question that many novels written by women are trying to answer: some in comic terms, some in tragic, some in speculative. We live in an unchartered world, as far as manners and morals are concerned, we are having to make up our own morality as we go. Our subject matter is enormous, there are whole new patterns to create. There is no point in sneering at women writers for writing of problems of sexual behaviour, of maternity, of gynaecology – those who feel the need to do it are actively engaged in creating a new pattern, a new blueprint.[22]

Drabble's early novels read more like sick-room charts than blueprints, but beginning with *The Waterfall* it is tempting to look in her novels for visions of female possibilities in a world still ordered by men. Drabble is not a political novelist. Although she believes that "political theory can produce very great works of art", she says "*I* can't do it. I don't want to do it . . . I just want to make a fairly modest statement about something very specific".[23] But there are revolutionary implications in the "modest statement" Drabble makes in *The Waterfall* about the possibilities of individual women's altering our situation. *The Waterfall* is not utopian. It does not envisage a new social order. It is much more exciting than that, because it suggests that women's liberation is not in our hands, but in our heads. Even within patriarchal institutions, playing the roles patriarchy has assigned us, women can absolutely, if quietly, refuse to be defined by those roles. It lies entirely within our power to heal our inner divisions and regard ourselves as whole, authentic, fully existent human beings.

This is the message of radical feminism, heralded by Virginia Woolf in *Three Guineas* and currently expounded by thinkers and poets like Mary Daly, Susan Griffin, and Adrienne Rich. Though muted, it informs the pages of *The Waterfall*, perhaps the most radically feminist of Drabble's books. Yet we must ask whether *The Waterfall* is a usable guidebook or blueprint for women, since there are two special conditions of Jane's situation that may make her success unique rather than exemplary.

Drabble herself has noted one of them. In her interview with Nancy Hardin, she calls *The Waterfall* "a wicked book" because it describes an experience "that is not universal", the experience of "sublime, romantic passion". Jane Gray is "saved from fairly pathological conditions by loving a man", and while most women have ample opportunities for heterosexual affairs, not many women meet a man like James Otford, an unreal and fantastic amalgam of Prince Charming and the demon lover. Even Drabble has to admit that "there's no guidance in [Jane's love story] for me. . . . As Doris Lessing would say, there are not all that many men in the world these days who are worth looking for. . . . And if a woman happens to meet one of the few men available, good luck to her. But I mean it's luck".

There is another respect in which Jane Gray is lucky. Like most of us, she fills a number of roles patriarchy has assigned women; she is wife, mother, mistress, and housewife. Unlike most of us, she is also an artist. And if it is through her extraordinary relationship with James Otford that she discovers her sexuality, it is through and by means of her art that she achieves integrity and autonomy. "I know why the caged bird sings", writes Maya Angelou. So do I. "Stone walls do not a prison make,/Nor iron bars a cage" for the poet Richard Lovelace because, "like committed linnets", he can sing.

Drabble's first novel is called *A Summer Bird-Cage*. It initiates her exploration of the situation of women locked in patriarchal cages. Does *The Waterfall* suggest that only the woman artist can achieve autonomy and transcendence, by mocking that cage with her song? I think, finally, not. I believe that as one novel succeeded another, Drabble came to perceive that the real cages are the ones we construct ourselves, as we internalize patriarchal thinking. *The Waterfall* suggests that "the mind is its own place, and in itself/Can make a heav'n of hell, a hell of heav'n". Art is only one form of mental liberation, and women who are not artists may still free themselves from the shackles of patriarchal thinking. Perhaps in order to test this hypothesis, Drabble turns from the extraordinary Jane Gray to write a novel about a woman who calls herself "an ordinary person".

NOTES

1 Determining whether or not there is such a genre and how it might differ from that essentially male paradigm Buckley outlines in *Seasons of Youth* is one of the challenging tasks facing feminist scholars.
2 Margaret Drabble, "Say a Good Word for the Curse", *Good Housekeeping* (English edition), February 1978, p. 51. I want to thank Charles T. Wood, of Dartmouth's history department, for drawing my attention to this article.
3 Patricia Meyer Spacks, *The Female Imagination* (New York: Alfred A. Knopf, 1975), p. 15.
4 Jean Leighton, *Simone de Beauvoir on Woman* (Rutherford, N. J.: Fairleigh Dickinson University Press, 1975), p. 31.
5 Ibid., p.32.
6 Ibid., p. 186.
7 Ibid., p. 34.
8 Ibid., p. 213.
9 "Say a Good Word for the Curse".
10 Margaret Drabble, *The Waterfall* (New York: Alfred A. Knopf, 1969), p. 3. Further references to W will occur in the text.
11 Moses Hadas, trans., Seneca's *Oedipus* (New York: The Liberal Arts Press, 1955), p. 6.
12 See, for instance, Beards, op. cit. or Libby, op. cit.
13 Mary Ellman, *Thinking About Women* (New York: Harcourt, Brace, 1978), p. 74.
14 As was Margaret Drabble in *Jerusalem the Golden*, by using a male genre borrowed from Arnold Bennett to shape her inchoate sense of the ambiguities of woman's situation.

[15] Joan Didion, "The Women's Movement", *The New York Times Book Review* (July 30, 1972), p. 14.
[16] Elaine Showalter, *A Literature of Their Own* (Princeton: Princeton University Press, 1977), p. 4.
[17] Sara deFord and Clarinda Harriss Lott, *Forms of Verse* (New York: Appleton–Century–Crofts, 1971), p. 323.
[18] Constance Ayers Denne and Katharine M. Rogers, "Women Novelists: A Distinct Group?" *Women's Studies*, Vol. 3, No. 1 (1975), 5–28.
[19] Hardin interview, op. cit.
[20] Margaret Drabble, "Revelations and Prophecies", *Saturday Review* (May 27, 1978), pp. 54, 56.
[21] Margaret Drabble, "Cassandra in a World Under Seige", *Ramparts*, Vol. 10, No. 8 (February 1972), 50–54.
[22] Margaret Drabble, "A Woman Writer", *Books*, No. 11 (Spring 1973), 4–6.
[23] Firchow, op. cit.

4 "Things that have never been written about": *The Needle's Eye*

When *The Needle's Eye* was published in 1972, it must have surprised readers who thought they knew to expect from Margaret Drabble another novel about the situation of being a woman. For the first paragraph situates the reader in the consciousness of a man, Simon Camish, from whose point of view a large bulk of the novel is narrated.

As she told early reviewers of the book, Drabble quite consciously attempted with it to enlarge her imaginative scope. "In *The Needle's Eye*, I've stepped rather nervously on to various floating icebergs, like writing at all about a man's job, which I have never dared to do before. And I had to work jolly hard to make sure that I got it plausible, let alone true, and that's stepping out of one's limits".[1] For the first time, Drabble prefaces a novel with an acknowledgement, to "all the lawyers who talked to me about this book". Simon Camish is a barrister, specializing in trade union law. The detail with which Drabble describes his work suggests strenuous research on her part – and also that her lawyer friends must have been not only helpful but very patient.

Of course this kind of research might just have produced what philosophers call "knowledge about" an alien subject, in this case "man". But the first paragraph of *The Needle's Eye* suggests what the rest of the novel confirms, that Drabble was also attempting to "know" Simon in all his human complexity:

He stood there and waited. He was good at that. There was no hurry. There was plenty of time. He always had time. He was a punctual and polite person, and that was why he was standing

71

there, buying a gift for his hostess. Politeness was an emotion –
could one call it an emotion, he wondered? that was how he
regarded it, certainly – an emotion that he both feared and
understood.[2]

One male reader of *The Waterfall* complained to me that "Margaret
Drabble sees men as pretty simple creatures, with mostly biologic
and social needs, in contrast to her deep, agonized, ambiguous,
ambivalent women".[3] The first pages of *The Needle's Eye* introduce a
man who is as introspective, contradictory, and intriguing as any of
Drabble's female protagonists – more so, in fact, than Clara
Maugham, whose background and upbringing are very similar to
his. Raised, like Clara, in a working class home in the north of
England by a fanatically self-righteous, socially aspiring mother,
Simon has achieved both wealth and status – like Clara, by sheer
force of will. Unlike her, however – and this is what makes him the
more interesting as well as the more sympathetic character – he
realizes the price he has paid for his success. Clara says "I am too full
of will to love", but it does not bother her much. Simon, on the other
hand, not only knows but regrets his emotional emasculation:

> He also thought that perhaps there was a natural progression, an
> inevitable progression, for people like himself, from his back-
> ground, who had grown up amidst too much physical intimacy –
> houses too small, settees too narrow, bedrooms too full, kisses
> (like his grandparents') too brutal and forceful – from this world
> they could only wish to grow apart, into the thinner air of non-
> touching, into larger rooms and spaces. And having reached this
> clear, empty space, they would wish once more to find touching,
> to find chosen, not accidental warmth, to find intimacy and
> contact. And it would no longer be possible, the world of touch
> would be lost for ever . . . (NE, p. 46).

But however interesting Simon may be, however believable, *The
Needle's Eye* is not Drabble's *Portrait of a Gentleman*. In fact, as she
recently confided, the novel she had in mind while writing *The
Needle's Eye* was *The Portrait of a Lady*.[4] Yet it is worth remembering
that in order to paint a portrait of Isabel Archer, James also drew
one of Ralph Touchett, who not only loves his cousin but observes
and is endlessly curious about her.

The Portrait of a Lady begins in a masculine milieu – three men are taking tea on the lawn of an English country house – which sets the scene for the lady who then takes centre stage. Similarly, *The Needle's Eye* begins in the interior landscape of Simon's mind, as an introduction to the novel's principal character, Rose Vassiliou. "I'm going to try to write about a man", Drabble told an interviewer, when she was in the initial stages of writing *The Needle's Eye*, "but I may give it up. I may have to introduce a woman character . . . later on".[5] "Giving up" presented her with what she regarded as a technical challenge:

> I've never before written a book with two main characters. What I wanted to do was to have the reader see what each felt about the other and where they had got each other wrong, which I admire tremendously in other people's books. It's something that really gives me a thrill when two characters are presented to you as solid people and you, the reader in the middle, can see them misunderstanding. I wanted very much to do that.[6]

Locating her omniscient narrator alternatively in Simon's and Rose's consciousness, Drabble does give the reader a seat in the middle. But from that seat, what the reader sees is not so much the two main characters misunderstanding each other, as Simon earnestly attempting and ultimately failing to understand Rose. "A man like him, how could he ever guess, correctly, at what she truly felt?" (NE, p. 363).

Although *The Needle's Eye* appears at first to be a radical departure from the kind of "women's novel" Drabble had written previously, it is the logical, almost necessary, sequel to *The Waterfall*, in which Drabble creates her first psychologically integrated heroine. If the early novels are, as Drabble has said they are, about the *situation* of being a woman, *The Needle's Eye* is about *being* a woman in a world of patriarchal ideologies and institutions. Simon Camish, belonging to and identified with that world, is to a large extent exiled from understanding Rose Vassilou's uniquely female way of being in the world.

In 1973, Margaret Drabble wrote, "There is no point in sneering at women writers for writing of problems of sexual behaviour, of maternity, of gynaecology – those who feel the need to do it are actively engaged in creating a new pattern, a new blueprint. This area of personal relationships verges constantly on the political: it is not a narrow backwater of introversion, it is the main current which is changing the daily quality of our lives".[7] Her early novels, whose subjects are sexual behaviour, maternity, and gynaecology, are anything but blueprints of liberation for women; instead they reveal the inadequacy of any "liberated" style of life as a way of expressing the plenitude of female being. *The Waterfall*, on the other hand, while its heroine remains ostensibly confined in the "feminine" roles of mother and lover, does seem to chart a new pattern for what the radical feminist philosopher, Mary Daly, would call "living on the boundary":

> The process [of liberation] involves the creation of new space, in which women are free to become who we are, in which there are real and significant alternatives to the prefabricated identities provided within the enclosed spaces of patriarchal institutions. As opposed to the foreclosed identity allotted to us within thos spaces, there is a diffused identity – an open road to discovery of the self and of each other. The new space is located always "on the boundary". Its centre is on the boundary of patriarchal institutions, such as churches, universities, national and in-ternational politics, families. Its centre is the lives of women, whose experience of becoming changes the very meaning of centre for us by putting it on the boundary of all that has been considered central.[8]

For various reasons which Nancy Chodorow has recently, brilliantly, anatomized, "the basic masculine sense of self is separate".[9] Thus, what characterizes all patriarchal institutions is separation between the self and the not-self. On the most fundamen-tal level, as Simone de Beauvoir long ago perceived, this expresses itself as sexual polarization: "humanity is male and man defines woman not as herself but as relative to him. . . . He is the Subject, he is the Absolute – she is the Other". Even when the male instinct to polarize is not expressed in specifically sexual terms, as it is in the most basic of patriarchal institutions, marriage, it is pervasive. Central to all patriarchal institutions is a dualistic split between subject and object, self and other, us and them, either/or.

But what if "it isn't either or at all?" What if, instead, "it's and, and, and, and, and, and?"[10] If men in our culture grow up defining themselves as separate and distinct from others, Chodorow says, women – from earliest infancy – experience themselves as connected with other persons and with nature. If patriarchal thinking is dualistic, matriarchal thinking might be holistic.

How this thinking might find institutional expression we cannot say, since we continue to live in a patriarchal society. ("I and most women are writing about things that have never been written about, really", Drabble has said.[11]) What we can say about patriarchal institutions, however, is that they do polarize and furthermore that they polarize power. One of the poles is always superior to the other. If the self is valued, then the other is devalued, as no one has shown more devastatingly than de Beauvoir, in *The Second Sex*.

As yet, then, liberation "only verges on the political". It is fundamentally ontological. Politically it may be invisible, since it has to do not so much with styles of life as with states of mind. Stay-at-home Jane Gray is more liberated than swinging Clara Maugham, who can only free herself from traditional notions of femininity by acting like a man. Exerting her will, Clara exercises power – over her own feelings and over others. She does not transcend patriarchal thinking, she enacts and reinforces it. In surrendering her will, on the other hand, Jane Gray is responding not to a power that emanates from the man, James Otford, but to the more powerful dictates of her own psyche. To the casual observer, she appears merely passive, docilely confined to a role subordinate to men, her lover and her child. In fact, she has discovered that within these roles, she can express her self, an integer defying division. Thus she lives, fully, vibrantly, and invisibly, on the boundary of the most fundamental of patriarchal institutions, the family.

What particularly interests me about *The Needle's Eye* is that in this novel, Drabble seems to suggest, through Rose, what it might be like to live on the boundary of other patriarchal institutions, such as religion and the law. At the same time, I must admit that *The Needle's Eye* is inherently and probably unintentionally ambiguous on this score. It all depends on your vantage point. To a feminist critic situated on the boundary of the novel, Rose appears quite unmistakeably to be moving away from patriarchy's definitions of what is central, to a new centre of her own designation. From another perspective, provided within the novel by Simon, Rose's behaviour is more difficult to interpret. Simon senses that Rose is "a whole person so entirely there and so fully existing" that it is "a

dreadful audacity" to think of loving her (NE, p. 214). Yet he
finally has the audacity to think he understands her according to his
own conceptual framework, which is ultimately and inescapably
patriarchal. The question the reader of this novel must answer is,
which of these vantage points is Margaret Drabble's?

2

Rose Vassiliou, *née* Bryanston, feels – understandably – that she has
"been struggling through legal nightmares all [her] life" (NE,
p. 33). When she was twenty, her parents made her a ward of court to
prevent her from marrying a Greek from Camden Town, whose
parents ran a travel agency and smuggled Greeks out of Cyprus on
the side. The day after her twenty-first birthday, she married him
and was promptly disinherited. Eleven years later, she divorced him
for cruelty and, as the novel opens, she is again involved in legal
wrangles, as Christopher Vassiliou has just reopened custody
proceedings for their three children. "I'm terrified of lawyers",
Rose confides to Simon (NE, p. 35), who remembers how her face
had "flickered and flinched" (NE, p. 21) when she discovered he
was a barrister.

Nevertheless, because of Christopher's actions, Rose needs a
lawyer, and she turns to Simon for advice, which she then finds
ridiculous. For instance, when Simon tells her that the court will
consider whether Christopher has adequate accommodation for the
children, because "the law takes a serious view of things like
accommodation", Rose comments: "Interesting, isn't it, things that
the law takes seriously. Like bruises and adultery. It's a kind of code,
I suppose, for what really goes on". Possibly because Simon answers
that "one has to have a code" (NE, pp. 72–73), Rose decides not to
tell him about what really goes on in her mind and heart: "there
were many kinds of evidence that were not of much use in court"
(NE, p. 113).

Christopher's case for custody rests on his contention that Rose,
who lives in a decaying house in a working-class neighbourhood, is
depriving their children of material benefits which he, now wealthy,
can offer them. Rose reflects on the spiritual benefits she finds in
living as she does and wonders, "what sort of defence would this
make in a court of law? And who was to set about reducing it to an
affidavit?" (NE, p. 149).

Rose considers that "the law . . . and its processes, far from drawing ends and lines and boundaries, were also self-perpetuating, that they, like blows, answered nothing, they solved none of the confusions of the heart and the demands of the spirit, but instead generated their own course of new offences, new afflictions, new perversions" (NE, pp. 181–182).

Simon, on the other hand, although he believes that justice is "dry" (NE, p. 44) and "stony" (NE, p. 30), argues that "the law as an institution . . . is admirable". Reversing the Biblical maxim, he insists that "it isn't the letter that kills and the spirit that giveth life at all, it's the other way round. The spirit kills and the letter gives life" (NE, p. 245). This belief gets him, at least once in his career as we observe it, into an uncomfortable position. Because he believes in the principle of the closed shop, Simon finds himself defending a corrupt union against a rebel worker, with whom his human and liberal sympathies are engaged (NE, pp. 238–240). Camish "can't see the trees for the wood", his boss says, and Simon has to acknowledge that in some sense he is right. Although he entered the legal profession because of the individuals – the trees – it exists to serve, Simon operates according to the principle that "those that have may not reject those that have not". This, for Simon, is "the wood in which the trees [grow]" (NE, p. 200). But the principle is so abstract, so impervious to particularization, that it leads Simon into "defending the wrong cause for the right reason" (NE, p. 239).

Wearied by the law, Rose announces to Simon that she wants to give up the custody case, and judicially he reminds her that it's not her case but Christopher's. "*You* can't give it up", Simon insists. "*He* would have to" (NE, p. 255). She counteracts with her personal, morally absolute conviction that Christopher is right: "I'm a hopeless mother, I know I am, I'm mean and mad and selfish, he's *right* about me, how can I defend myself when he's right". And Simon answers, "with a fitting [i.e., legal] note of exasperation" that that's beside the point: no court in the country would take the children from the mother and give them to the father:

"Ah yes," she said, gazing at him, with a mysterious, mad, perverse, elevated smile upon her face, a smile quite awful in its unnatural dignity, "ah yes, but I *give* them, you remember, I *give* them."

The adjectives describing Rose's appearance here are filtered through Simon's patriarchal perspective. To the legal mind, there is something "unnatural" about Rose's attention to the trees and disregard for the forest.

This confrontation, in Simon's office, between the principled justice of the law and the demands of personal morality is short-circuited by Christopher's quixotic and unpredictable abduction of the children. Having taken them, as in his legal right, for the Easter holiday, he sends Rose a telegram announcing that he is in fact taking them out of the country. Thus, despite Rose's intention to circumvent the law, Christopher calls down upon himself its inexorable processes, as an injunction is served and Rose's solicitor remarks with complacent satisfaction to Simon, "as for the custody case, [Christopher's] done himself in completely" (NE, p. 278).

Of course he's right. "The case came up before Mr. Justice Menzies in three weeks' time, as had been predicted, and Mr. Justice Menzies, who did not much care for Rose, nevertheless found himself obliged" to deny Christopher's petition for custody (NE, p. 353). Proof, seemingly, of Simon's belief that "the letter gives life", that the legal process will guarantee "justice".

But Rose has a different definition of justice. "The decisions of judges", she maintains, "even when in her favour, were irrelevant: they chalked up no victory":

The confrontation (ah, this was it) could not end in victory, because it was a fight in which there was no winning. Some other resolution would have to be made, in which victory and defeat played no part, in which the boundaries did not enclose the spoils of war, and were not drawn by neutral external treaty and convention (NE, p. 182).

Rose rejects the language and the concepts of patriarchy. Refusing to accept as central the polarities of victory vs. defeat, justice vs. injustice, Rose re-centres herself on the boundary of the law. Accepting the judge's verdict, as she must, she nonetheless ignores it. The law says she cannot give her children to their father because she has won them. Rose transcends this just decision of the courts by the simple expedient of inviting Christopher to be her husband again, thus giving him his children without giving them up. Her friends are amazed and exasperated by her refusal to accept her victory and the spoils of the legal war.

All her friends, that is, except Simon. Acknowledging that "in some terms" Rose is talking "nonsense" when she says she wants to give up the case and her exclusive claim to the children, Simon nevertheless maintains that "it had made sense to him" (NE, p. 265). Identified, by profession and conviction, with the patriarchal institution of the law, Simon has moments of transcendent intuition which make him more able than any of Rose's other friends to understand her.

Rose puts her finger on the reason for this: "there was either religion or self-denial in his background . . . or he would not at all have known what she was talking about" (NE, p. 79). The religion in Simon's background explains both why he is a lawyer and why he loves and admires Rose for eluding the meshes of the law. Simon was brought up on the Old Testament, with its harsh doctrine of the inexorable consequences of Original Sin, summed up for him by the 137th psalm, whose "message was that the sins of the fathers shall be visited upon the children" (NE, p. 23). But Old Testament religion suggests a way of redeeming this bleak situation. Since man's nature is fallen, God will mercifully give him a set of laws to regulate his natural propensity for evil. Law does not, nor does it even claim to, transform human nature. But it can protect us from each other and make civilized life possible. Hence Simon's performance of "the laborious, technical, tedious, legal" (NE, p. 13) acts of his profession stems from a "religious" impulse.

But because Simon has also read the New Testament, he sees the limitations of the law. In the absence of the spirit (of love or justice), the letter protects, but cannot give, life. Moderating without modifying human nature, the law does not lead to salvation.

Like *The Portrait of a Lady*, *The Needle's Eye* – as its title suggests – is about wealth. It is also and more fundamentally an exploration of "the possibility of living, today, without faith, a religious life".[12] Simon's introspection, in the opening pages of the novel, reveals that he is deeply concerned with religious questions. Sitting in his host's living room, despising his fellow guests, Simon knows that although "one could order one's features and one's responses so [hatred] did not show, so that it caused no positive offence . . . that was no salvation: one might behave impeccably, and still, if one had not charity, it would be of no avail. And he no longer had any charity, it had all dried up in him" (NE, p. 11).

Because of his spiritual aridity, Rose becomes important to Simon. For Rose Vassiliou, born an heiress, has "given all her money away to the poor, or something ridiculous like that" (NE,

p. 15). This is all Simon knows about Rose, when he meets her at
the dinner party which opens the novel, but it is enough to make
her appear to him in terms of religious iconography. "She looked,
because of age and softness, authentic, as ancient frescoes look in
churches, frescoes which in their very dimness offer a promise of
truth that a more brilliant (however beautiful) restoration denies"
(NE, p. 17). Driving Rose to her shabby home, Simon listens to her
speak what sounds to his ears like the language of religion. "Don't
you find [this neighborhood] depressing?" he asks her. "I hated it at
first", she concedes. "I hated it for years, but I believed in it, and
now I love it. . . . All this, you see, I created it for myself. Stone by
stone and step by step. I carved it out, I created it by faith, I
believed in it, and then very slowly, it began to exist. And now it
exists. It's like God. It requires faith. . . . If you see what I mean".
"I don't see what you mean", Simon replies, "but it's quite
astonishing to hear you say it" (NE, pp. 35–36).

Another astonishing thing, to Simon, about Rose is that her
middle name is "Vertue". He resolves to ask her about it and is
pleased when she tells him that, although it is just a family name, she
has taken it seriously. Taught as a child to believe literally in the
parable that says it is easier for a camel to get through a needle's eye
than for a rich man to get into heaven, Rose made a "solemn vow"
(NE, p. 75) never to possess anything she feared to lose. Twenty
years later, she kept her vow, giving away the legacy of £30,000 her
grandfather had bequeathed her. "What else in life should one ever
seek for but a sense of being right?" Rose asks, and Simon replies,
enviously but humbly, "I wish that I too could arrive at such a state
of grace" (NE, p. 101).

As he gets to know Rose, Simon feels "nothing less than a re-birth
in his nature" (NE, p. 154). Only Biblical language will express his
feeling. Knowing Rose is "like a new contract, like the rainbow after
the flood" (NE, p. 216). Like the Israelites, Simon feels he is
entering the promised land: "he was entering into her own land, her
realities would become real for him, he too would have to stand
there" (NE, p. 205).

Rose represents the new covenant which will supersede the old,
love which will make the law irrelevant. She becomes for Simon the
mystical rose, "an everlasting flower, never to open, never to die, a
witness, a signal, a heroic pledge" (NE, p. 70). When, in his office,
she makes her gesture of ultimate renunciation – she will give the
children to Christopher – she stands "irradiated" for Simon (NE,

p. 259). It is almost inevitable, then, that Simon will interpret her circumvention of the law in taking Christopher back as a gesture of selfless renunciation motivated by religious belief. Rose need not fear, as she does, that "he, like others, would think that she had gained more than she had lost" (NE, p. 364). On the contrary, Simon believes "she is winning some [spiritual] victory in there, behind those threadbare curtains" *because* "she is sticking it out, meaninglessly faithful she is loyal to her vows" (NE, p. 356). In fact, his only worry is that she may be getting soft, that she may not be renouncing enough. "He watched the inside of her house, the rooms of it, the rooms she lived in. Breathlessly, over the years, he watched. They changed, a little. They did not change much. Such love, such salvation, he felt, at the sight of each object that remained in its place. The tea caddy. The tin tray. The armchair. The shabby cat" (NE, p. 359). He is alarmed to discover her wearing a fur coat and almost ludicrously relieved to realize that it's only "a moth-eaten old thing she had picked up at a jumble sale" (NE, p. 360). His final vision of Rose is an apotheosis of the moth-eaten:

> The light fell from the windows, the winter sun fell on to her pale hair, shafts and slanting planes of it, and he could see all the dusty motes in the bright air, and her hair itself, falling on to the points of her fur collar, fell into a thousand bright individual fiery sparks, the hair and the fur meeting, radiant, luminous, catching whatever fell from the sun upon them, stirring like living threads in the sea into a phosphorescent life, turning and lifting, alive on the slight breeze of her walking, a million lives from the dead beasts, a million from her living head, haloed there, a million shining in a bright and dazzling outline, a million in one. She walked ahead, encircled by brightness . . . (NE, p. 363).

Observing Rose provides Simon his closest approximation to a religious experience, "an encounter with a power beyond the appearances of things, persons, and events".[13] But because he conceptualizes Rose in Christian terms, he cannot perceive that she herself is undergoing a religious crisis. Rose's most strenuous efforts in this novel are directed towards creating a livable space for herself on the boundary of religion which, like the law, is a patriarchal institution.

Hypostatizing transcendent Being, patriarchal religions like Christianity establish a dichotomy between the self and the other

("God"). Moreover, this polarization distributes power unequally. The self is powerless (and worthless) in respect to the Other, with Whom one may be atoned only by transcending – in effect, by denying – one's self. For women, of course, this is a metaphysical reenactment of the sexual polarization that prevails in patriarchy, since Christianity hypostatizes God as an omnipotent male.[14]

Rose seems at times to be attempting to create on the boundary of Christianity a non-hypostatic religion, in which religious experience is not a relationship between her self and a personification of transcendent Otherness, but a realization of the creative potential for Being within her self.[15] To succeed, she would, of course, have to redefine transcendence, learn not to deny but to affirm her self. She would have to learn to accept – and even to celebrate – "in herself, the natural shortcomings of humanity" (NE, p. 141). And to do so, she would first have to exorcise "the internalized patriarchal presence, which carries with it feelings of guilt, inferiority, and self-hatred".[16]

Like Simon's, Rose's definition of righteousness derives from the traditional religious education she received as a child. From the Bible she learned that it is easier for a camel to go through the eye of a needle than for a rich man to enter heaven. Internalizing the impossible example of Christ, she yearns to renounce. She gives away her inherited wealth and builds up "brick by brick the holy city of her childhood, the holy city in the shape of that patched subsiding house" (NE, p. 53) in north London, where she lives in relative poverty. But she is wracked with feelings of guilt, inferiority, and self-hatred because she has not renounced everything. "I gave some money away," she tells Simon, "but that's nothing. There are still plenty of things I wouldn't like to part with. The children, for instance" (NE, pp. 75–76).

Responding to the religious imperative she has internalized, Rose enters Simon's office with her mind made up: "I must learn to give up. It's so hard, it's so hard, but there's no other way" the internalized presence of patriarchal religion offers Rose of transcendence. For the religion she has been taught tells her that in striving to become atoned with the Other, she must deny her self and its desires. Perceived accurately by Simon, Rose makes an ecstatically selfless gesture of renunciation in offering to give up her children to Christopher:

"Ah yes," she said, gazing at him, with a mysterious, mad,

perverse, elevated smile upon her face, a smile quite awful in its unnatural dignity, "ah yes, . . . I *give* them, you remember, I *give* them."

Thus this gesture, which circumvents the rules of one patriarchal institution – the law – fulfills those of another, religion.

Hypostatizing God provides images, models for behaviour. Rose has acted all her life in response to these images, or what she calls her "visions":

> She had seen herself marrying Christopher [thus disinheriting herself] . . . and it was vision that had walked her to the registry office: the image of herself doing it had been too strong for her. Then again, later, she had seen herself signing the cheque [giving away her grandfather's legacy]. She had seen her hand writing her signature. God, she thought, had held her hand (NE, p. 262).

In a coffee shop, having declared to Simon that she will give the children to Christopher, Rose has another vision, of herself in Africa, having renounced not only children but home and probably health in the service of "God". "It was a vision so strong, so real, that she knew she must do it":

> I will voyage into that dark interior, I will satisfy this spiritual craving, I will see what it is like, that other world, the world of destitution, I was made for it, and there, in that hideous dark misery, which now, here, I cannot imagine, but which there could not deny itself to me – for what else would there be, nothing, nothingness – there I should see it, the unimaginable. It is there, it calls me, I have only to walk towards it, I myself. It is in me to go that journey, so how can I refuse it? . . . I cannot survive my own rejection of this image. It gathers in the darkness of my soul. It is my only chance to appease God himself, who so pursues me with these suggestions, who sends after me his fierce angels with their clattering wings. It is sacrifices that God has always demanded. He demanded Isaac. On the hilltop, the innocent. He shall have my children. On that dingy airport, where I shall be ill, and wretched, and lonely, he shall have myself. And there I shall find him. It is the only way to find him (NE, pp. 262–263).

In quest of atonement, Rose – like the saints before her – is prepared to travel the way of abnegation, denying her self to be united with the Other.

What ensues is the first exorcism. Recognizing by some grace beyond the reach of religion that the God she has hypostatized is nothing more than an internalization of the patriarchal religion she has been taught, she plays out a psychomachia on the stage of her own mind, which she feels is "divided" between the imaginary woman in the African airport and the real woman in the coffee shop:

> You realise, of course, what you've done, said Rose, mother of three children, to that unpleasant martyr, that faithless missionary. You've simply constructed for yourself the most horrible renunciation your mind can conceive. That's all you've done. It's silly, it's pointless.
>
> But the woman in the airport looked up from her dusty shoes, with a tight dismissive smile of contempt, and said No, no. I didn't construct it. Christopher and God constructed it, they connived at it, they left me nothing else to do, don't you remember?
>
> I don't believe you, said Rose.
>
> Ah, said the woman. Refuse to believe. Abandon me. The choice is yours.
>
> Oh God, said Rose, munching her salad angrily. I don't care. You can die for all I care. I'm going to go back now, and soon I can collect Maria and Marcus from school.
>
> And the woman rose to her feet, white and wailing. In Rose's mind she wailed, like a soul in hell. On the bottom right-hand corner of the day of judgement she wept and wrung her hands, across the continents (NE, pp. 264–265).

Heretofore in Drabble's fiction, division of the self has been seen as pathological. Healing that division, Jane Gray becomes Drabble's first whole person. Here, however, division is the necessary first step towards integration. Rose must relocate the other. If it is not external to her, if there is no hypostatized God but only her internalization of the mandates of patriarchal religion, then she can exorcise it and assert her self, which will expand to fill the space once occupied by the Other.

Rose's immediate course of action is to wait. She will not obey her religious impulse to renounce her children, and in practical terms, she cannot, because in abducting the children, Christopher takes away her option to do so. Her response to his action is initially passive; she allows the solicitors and barristers and judges to issue their injunction and goes home to await the outcome. There she receives a phone call from her eldest son, who tells her that Christopher is taking the children simply to the Bryanstons' estate in Norfolk. Passive still, Rose accepts Simon's suggestion that they drive to Norfolk to get the children and bring them home.

At Branston Hall, however, Rose does more than collect her children. She evokes the last ghost of patriarchal religion, John Bunyan, and exorcises him, thus freeing herself for genuine transcendence.

With a sense that something "significant" awaits her, Rose leaves Simon with Christopher in her parents' living room and goes to her bedroom, where she finds her "nursery copy" of *Pilgrim's Progress*, "that fierce companion, that bitter solace" of her lonely childhood, which enacts one of the great transcendence myths of Christianity, the journey from alienation to atonement. "What shall I do to be saved, Pilgrim had said. It had been her favourite book. The journeys, the hazards, the faith-created mirage of a heavenly city", so like the one Rose has built for herself in north London. Beside *Pilgrim's Progress* on the shelf stands Bunyan's spiritual autobiography, *Grace Abounding*, in which Rose had heavily underscored passages that had seemed to express her own conviction of sin: "Oh, how happy now, was every creature over what I was; for they stood fast and kept their station, but I was gone and lost":

> Gone and lost, gone and lost. Yes, that was the way it had been. How easy it was to underestimate what had been endured. . . . For years of my life, Rose thought, I remember it now, I would have changed places with any living thing. . . . How slowly I learned to live, to make myself forget (NE, p. 330).

Imbued with Bunyan's sense that the self is worthless in respect to the transcendent Other, Rose had learned that the way to salvation is by renunciation. Her true spiritual progress, however, is the path of acceptance, which involves renouncing Bunyan and the ecstacy of self-abnegation.

Rose sets foot on this path when she leaves her bedroom and her brooding to "go and see if the children were asleep, and have a look round to see how their room had been decorated. She had been wanting to do that all evening, on one level, on her most ordinary functional level, but had been too depressed and waylaid by Bunyan. To hell with Bunyan, she said to herself . . ."(NE, p. 334). Consigning "poor Bunyan" to hell, Rose takes a step on her journey toward the boundary of religion. Bunyan's self-abnegation, his sense of worthlessness in relation to a distant and perfect God, is – as Rose can now see – neurotic (NE, p. 329). Moreover, it does not even transcend the self. By making his self the object of his anxious scrutiny, Bunyan exalted it in importance. Puritanical self-abasement is a subtle form of idolatry.

By shaking off her morbid preoccupation with the state of her soul, Rose genuinely transcends her self. She also lays the foundation for transcending religious dualism. For if she acts according to the dictates of her "most ordinary functional" self, she will no longer be obeying the internalized dictates of some hypostatized Other. By trusting her instincts, Rose would relocate and rename God. No longer an icon, an impossible model to emulate, God would now be understood as creative energy. "Why", Mary Daly asks, "must 'God' be a noun? Why not a verb – the most active and dynamic of all", Be-ing?[17] Genuine transcendence means realizing that wherever and whenever one's self *is*, in the fulness of its being, one is atoned with the Divine.

But while this is the logical last step in the journey Rose has begun toward transcending patriarchal religion, it is not clear at the end of *The Needle's Eye* that she has decisively taken it. For, ironically, what enables her to reject Bunyan is her acceptance not so much of herself as of Christopher. "Never, since she first met Christopher," Rose reflects, has she felt "gone and lost". "What freakish providence had given her Christopher", she wonders, "so obsessed by the thought of possession that he refused to let her reject him? His desire to grab – herself, children, money, even parents-in-law – had proved too strong for her will to renounce" (NE, p. 333). If this was true when Rose was eighteen, it is no less true now. Christopher, whose name means "bearing Christ", is more powerful than Rose.[18] "Rose looked at Christopher: really, she thought, in the end, one had just got to take him, and that's that. Her spirit, for the first time in years, moved to acceptance . . ."(NE, p. 304)

In accepting Christopher, then, Rose is *not* affirming her most ordinary, functional self. She is simply substituting one (male) authority figure for another, and for the same reason. Bunyan's theology promises atonement with the Divine ground of being as the reward for self-denial. When Rose's "spirit" moves to accept Christopher, she imagines that "it might one day rise and reach and settle in the clearer air"(NE, p. 304).

So motivated, Rose takes Christopher back to live with her and discovers, to her dismay, that "she had never made that leap into the clearer air":

> Her whole nature was being corrupted by her deep resistance to Christopher, by the endless, sickening struggle to preserve something of her own. . . . She looked back with bitter regret to those exhausting days of peace, when she was on her own, alone, lonely, when she would put the children to bed and then sit up herself a little while with a book, and then go quietly to bed. They seemed endowed, those days, with a spiritual calm that it had been a crime to lose (NE, pp. 364–365).

Both Simon and Rose see her decision to take Christopher back as a denial of her self on behalf of "the others" (NE, p. 365), of Christopher and the children. But while this represents a religious victory to Simon, it is a religious defeat for Rose. She is waylaid on her journey to the boundary of patriarchal religion by a regressive detour to the centre of that primary patriarchal institution, marriage. Acting in response to Christopher's power, she denies not only her self-interest but her self, her very nature.

Simon thinks that nature had made Rose "unremarkable, an ordinary person: fate had capriciously elected her to notoriety: and she had made the painful journey back to nature by herself, alone, guided by nothing but her own knowledge, against the current" (NE, p. 299). Here, as so often, he is almost right. Her journey *is* back to nature, her own nature. But she doesn't make it all the way.

Simon always associates Rose with nature. "The images that gathered round and above her were emanations, simple risings and gatherings from the soft, full lake of her nature" (NE, p. 175). So does Drabble, associating Rose with wild flowers, specifically with the London Rocket, "a modest and unattractive little plant" that "grows on waste patches" in the blighted cities that are man's "improvement" on nature (NE, p. 218).[19]

"I don't know what my images mean", Drabble has said, "but I know they mean something fairly involved to me and I use them because I don't know what I mean in words".[20] Perhaps it is

because she doesn't know quite what she means to say about Rose
that Drabble gives the task of explaining her to Simon, a man. *The
Needle's Eye* might have been a very different book had it been
narrated from the point of view of Rose's friend, Emily, who
"recognized" in Rose's collection of pressed wildflowers "her true
history". Rose meets Emily when she goes away to school and even
then the older girl intuitively understands when Rose tells her why
she collects flowers. "I did it for fun when I was six", Rose confides.
"I was quite happy then I think. I think. It got worse later".

> "Ah yes," said Emily, "it does. . . . It gets worse and worse and
> worse. You're quite right. You're the first person I've ever met
> who actually *admitted* it. But shall I tell you something? Shall I tell
> you something? It doesn't go on getting worse for ever. There
> comes a point when it gets better and better."

"How do you know?" Rose challenges, and Emily answers, "I know
because I've made my mind up. I'm not going to put up with it. You
wait and see. And you won't put up with it either" (NE, p. 222).
    This is a woman's conversation,[21] in which much is said by being
left unsaid. "It" is the life women live in patriarchal society, and as
any woman knows, it gets worse and worse the older one grows.
Emily, more radical than Rose, vows that she will not put up with it.
And she "hears" Rose saying, with her collection of wild flowers,
that she won't put up with it either. Collecting wild flowers, Rose is
symbolically collecting and preserving her self from a patriarchal
society which uproots all that is natural and replaces it with laws,
institutions, cities, and culture.[22]
    I can imagine another conversation between Rose and Emily,
one that does not take place in this book. What if Emily, rather than
Simon, had heard Rose's explanation of why she loves the
neighbourhood she lives in?

> I hated it for years, but I believed in it, and now I love it. . . . All
> this, you see, I created it for myself. Stone by stone and step by
> step. I carved it out, I created it by faith, I believed in it, and then
> very slowly, it began to exist. And now it exists. It's like God. It
> requires faith. . . . If you see what I mean.

"I don't see what you mean", Simon says. I think Emily would
have. Where Simon heard the language of Christianity (belief, love,

faith, God), Emily would have heard the radical language of post-Christian theology, where God is a verb. Rose is saying, for those with ears to hear, that she is affirming and celebrating her own creative energy – "I created it for myself. Stone by stone and step by step. I carved it out, I created it by faith, I believed in it, and then very slowly, it began to exist". Perhaps what Simon doesn't see is that the antecedent of "it" in Rose's statement that "it's like God" is not a noun but a verb. "It" is affirming, creating, *be-ing*. And Emily would understand that "it" *is* "like God".

Had this conversation taken place, *The Needle's Eye* might have ended differently, for Emily doubtless would not only have understood but encouraged Rose to continue to assert her self. Drabble doesn't tell us what Emily thinks of Rose's decision to take Christopher back, but I imagine she would agree with Rose that "she had done it in the dry light of arid generosity" (NE, p. 365). "The fascination of what's difficult", says Drabble in her epigraph to *The Needle's Eye*, quoting Yeats, "Has dried the sap out of my veins, and rent/My heart from all its natural content". At the end of *The Needle's Eye*, Rose has become, as Emily would see, the final pressed flower in her collection.

Both Simon and Christopher sense the importance of Emily's friendship to Rose. Christopher unconsciously acknowledges the subversiveness of female bonding against patriarchy when he cites "infidelity with Emily" in his divorce case, although "there was no sexual element to create offense" (NE, p. 223). Less thoroughly identified with patriarchy than Christopher, Simon simply says that "they could not have survived without each other" (NE, p. 360). Moreover, he does not feel threatened by Rose and Emily but attracted to them:

> How agreeable, how extremely agreeable the two women looked. They looked – he found it hard to explain it to himself – they looked complete, they looked like people. So many women, he found, did not look like people at all: they aspired after some image other than the personal . . . provocative, female, other (NE, pp. 213–214).

Simon's response to Rose and Emily confirms Mary Daly's assertion that women living on the boundary of patriarchy exude power, "not political power in the usual sense but rather a flow of healing energy which is participation in the power of being".[23] But Simon has difficulty finding words to express this power of being that emanates from Rose and Emily. And he, not Emily, is Margaret Drabble's surrogate in the novel. Like him, Drabble seems to sense that Emily is and that Rose might become a whole person. Like him, she finds it hard to explain and harder to accept.

Rose understands why Christopher resents her friendship with Emily. "How could one not resent the natural flowing of a resilient, indestructible personal joy? Such things must not be spoken of, they must not be admitted". (NE, p. 223). She might have been speaking not of Christopher but of her creator, Margaret Drabble, who will neither give Emily a voice nor allow Rose to complete her journey to liberation. Indeed, she insists that Rose does not even *want* "freedom or liberation".[24]

Feminist critics, as Drabble herself notes, see Rose's decision to take Christopher back as "some kind of sell-out".[25] Drabble's own views on the novel's ending are, at best, confused. When Nancy Hardin asked her whether Rose "loses her sense of grace in the end when she chooses to stay with Christopher and the children", Drabble answered equivocally: on the one hand she said, "I don't think she could lose it really"; on the other, she had to admit that Rose "loses her peace of mind", and that "perhaps she does lose her sense of grace just slightly". Finally, intriguingly, she said that she "might not have made it end" as it does if she and her husband, from whom she is now divorced, hadn't still been living together.

In the novel, Rose is prevented from completing her journey to the boundary of patriarchal religion because she voluntarily returns to the not-so-tender trap of patriarchal marriage. Whether or not the same causal relationship applies to Drabble, it is clear that she has not got much further than Simon in her ideas about what constitutes religious experience. "I see Rose", she has said, "in very simple religious terms. She's a girl who hungers and thirsts after righteousness . . ."[26] In an afterword to Monica Mannheimer's article on *The Needle's Eye*, Drabble cautions that "it would be a mistake to underrate Rose's genuine sense of the religious life as a source of motivation in her, for I have tried to portray it as real rather than neurotic". What kind of religious life Drabble sees as real, rather than neurotic, is clear from her next statement: "Rose, *like Bunyan*, is prepared to make a bet on the existence of God" (emphases mine). "I can't really accept", she recently told an interviewer,[27] "that oneself is necessarily the most important person. Of course, you've got to be O.K.; you've got to love yourself before you can love anybody. But that isn't the end of it. Loving yourself isn't the end of the road. You've got to do something with it, and that, I think, is religion". Is it Christianity? "It's not traditional Christianity. I'm not a churchgoer; I could never say the creed with any confidence whatsoever. I do think there are certain concepts of Christianity that mean a great deal to me. Maybe I was brought up with it, and it's hard to get rid of if you're brought up with it. But the concept of loving your neighbour and putting up with the unlovely people and trying not to think of yourself are important to me".

Like Rose, Drabble has regressed. This statement reflects the kind of confusion we saw in *Jerusalem the Golden* between two kinds of freedom. Anyone reading *Beyond God the Father* and other feminist theology will see that there is no conflict between loving others and loving oneself. "You've got to love yourself before you can love anybody". Drabble's statement implies that loving others is more important than loving oneself and that loving oneself is important only as the necessary preliminary step to the greater good of loving others. Thus it not only makes the patriarchal religious distinction between self and other but reiterates the patriarchal system of values, whereby other is better than self. Feminist theology, on the other hand, sees the relationship between loving oneself and loving others as simultaneous and reciprocal. Loving myself, I am affirming the creative power of being in all my sisters and brothers. Becoming myself, I affirm human becoming.[28]

The Needle's Eye will disappoint some readers because Drabble does not seem aware of, or will not acknowledge, its hidden agenda of women's liberation. Yet it is there, sabotaging Drabble's intentions and – to my mind – enriching her novel.

"I have never had very high expectations of happiness," Drabble has said, in writing about *The Needle's Eye*. And, discussing the Yeats epigraph with one reviewer, she said that it applied to Rose and Simon, " 'who all their lives had done what they ought to do and not what they wanted to' do, and so could no longer take any spontaneous joy in doing anything. 'On the other hand,' she [said], 'why the hell should we be able to? Why should one have any natural content in life?' "[29] In her next novel, Margaret Drabble will ask "why not?"

NOTES

[1] John Clare, "Margaret Drabble's Everyday Hell", (London) *Times* (March 27, 1972), p. 6.
[2] Margaret Drabble, *The Needle's Eye* (New York: Alfred A. Knopf, 1972), p. 3. Further references to NE will appear in the text.
[3] Personal communication from Jay Martin, 1978,
[4] Dee Preussner, "Interview with Margaret Drabble", forthcoming in *Modern Fiction Studies*. My thanks to the author for letting me see a typescript of this interview before its publication.
[5] Firchow, op. cit.
[6] Clare, op. cit.
[7] "The Woman Writer," op. cit.
[8] Mary Daly, *Beyond God the Father: Toward a Philosophy of Women's Liberation* (Boston: Beacon Press, 1973), pp. 40–41.
[9] Nancy Chodorow, *The Reproduction of Mothering: Psychoanalysis and the Sociology of Gender* (Berkeley: University of California Press, 1978), p.169. See also Dorothy Dinnerstein, *The Mermaid and the Minotaur: Sexual Arrangements and Human Malaise* (New York: Harper & Row, 1976) for anticipatory corroboration of Chodorow's account of how our culture creates gender identity. Dinnerstein's orientation is both psychoanalytic and existentialist, building on the initial perceptions of Freud and de Beauvoir.
[10] Doris Lessing, *Briefing for a Descent into Hell* (New York: Alfred A. Knopf, 1971), p. 165.
[11] Poland, op. cit.
[12] "The Author Comments", op. cit.
[13] *Beyond God the Father*, p. 81.
[14] See *Beyond God the Father*, chapter one. Several essays in *Womanspirit Rising* (op. cit.) elaborate the argument of this paragraph, as does Naomi R. Goldenberg in *Changing of the Gods: Feminism and the End of Traditional Religions* (Boston: Beacon Press, 1979).
[15] *Beyond God the Father*, p. 29.
[16] Ibid., p. 50
[17] Ibid., pp. 33–34.
[18] Respecting Christ, women should reflect that so long as we remain dependent on God the Father and his Son, our Big Brother, we will remain children in the Family of Man (which will remain just that). See Naomi Goldenberger's intelligent extension of Freud's concern (in *Totem and Taboo* and *Moses and Monotheism*) for the Oedipal sons to the even more disadvantaged patriarchal daughters in *Changing of the Gods*, chapter three, "Oedipal Prisons."
[19] For speculation that is taking place on the frontiers of feminist thinking, about the relationship between women and nature, see Mary Daly, *Gyn/Ecology: the Metaethics of Radical Feminism* (Boston: Beacon Press, 1978) and Susan Griffin, *Woman and Nature: the Roaring inside Her* (New York: Harper & Row, 1978).
[20] Hardin interview, op. cit.
[21] Cf. Phyllis Chesler on women's conversations: "Many dialogues between women seem 'senseless' or 'mindless' to men. Two women talking often seem to be reciting monologues at each other, neither really listening to (or 'judging')

what the other is saying. Two personal confessions, two sets of feelings, seem to be paralleling one another, rather 'mindlessly,' and without 'going anywhere'. In fact, what the women are doing – or where they are 'going' – is toward some kind of emotional resolution and comfort. Each woman comments upon the other's feelings by reflecting them in a very sensitive matching process. . . . A very special prescience is at work here. On its most ordinary level, it affords women a measure of emotional reality and a kind of comfort that they cannot find with men. On its highest level, it constitutes the basic tools of art and psychic awareness". *Women and Madness* (New York: Doubleday, 1972), p. 268.

22 For elaboration of this point see Sherry B. Ortner, "Is Female to Male as Nature is to Culture?" in *Woman, Culture, and Society*, ed. Michelle Zimbalist Rosaldo and Louise Lamphere (Stanford: Stanford University Press, 1974), pp. 67–87.

23 *Beyond God the Father*, p. 41.

24 "The Author Comments", op. cit.

25 Ibid.

26 Hardin interview, op. cit.

27 Preussner interview, op. cit.

28 See *Beyond God the Father*, p. 35. Perhaps it is because radical feminist philosophy and theology are grounded in existentialism that Drabble seems both attracted to and suspicious of them. Cf. Sarah and Simone.

29 Coleman, op. cit.

5 "A new pattern, a new blueprint": *The Realms of Gold*

The first character we meet in *The Realms of Gold* is an octopus who lives "in a square plastic box with holes for his arms".[1] This mute creature speaks for the condition of all the principal characters of the novel. Frances Wingate, the central protagonist, loves the octopus she sees on a visit to a marine research laboratory for "its gray fleshy body, its lovely tinted iridescent gray muscles, its faint blushes and changes, its round suckers, its responsiveness, its sensibility, its grace" (RG, p. 18). And she marvels that "the octopus, intelligent creature that he was, could survive in a plastic box" (RG, p. 6).

Janet Bird, her distant cousin, who has doubtless never visited a marine research laboratory, nonetheless thinks of an octopus when she looks at her infant son, miserable with teething: "He waved his octopus hands . . . He looked at her and moaned. She could do nothing, nothing. It's no use looking at *me*, she said, desperately, aloud" (RG, p. 133). For Janet herself is barely surviving in her little box of a development house, married unhappily to a man who works "at a plastics factory" (RG, p. 156).

Frances's nephew Stephen has a baby too, which he takes "as seriously as a mother octopus would its many offspring" (RG, p. 12). But mother octopuses who live in plastic boxes don't have many offspring. "The male octopus hadn't known his limitations", Frances thinks. "He thought he could have a full, active, healthy life in that box, or surely he would have sat down and died?" (RG, p. 7). The female octopus knows better: "the female of the species died, invariably, after giving birth" (RG, p. 6). Adopting the female's wisdom along with her role, Stephen kills himself and his baby because "the conditions of survival were so dreadful that it was undignified to survive" (RG, p. 88).

The octopus, with its fleshy body, its responsiveness, its sensibility, its grace, is confined in a box made of plastic. So confined, it is isolated from others of its kind. In the language of metaphor, Drabble is saying that life in technological society is unnatural and deadly. This novel goes further than *The Needle's Eye* in condemning patriarchy. It also goes further in imagining a woman who breaks free from its unnatural constraints. As the novel opens, Frances Wingate, like the male octopus, is surviving rather nicely in a plastic box, which is how she thinks of her hotel room. But only temporarily. "She never understood people who said they felt submerged by hotel rooms, that they felt extinguished, annihilated, depersonalized. She had occasionally felt the reverse – that herself, suddenly put down in transit, was so powerful that it might burst through the frail partition walls and send all the things swirling" (RG, p. 3). Asserting herself, Frances – unlike Rose Vassiliou – makes it out of her plastic box all the way back to nature. And what she discovers there suggests that Drabble's vision in this novel is gynocentric.

The plot of *The Realms of Gold* has little to do with this vision and, moreover, is almost impossible to summarize intelligibly. What are probably most apparent are its contrivances, the various coincidences which seem to account for the sequence of events. These raise vexing and crucial questions, to which I will return. But for the time being, I want simply to make two observations about this improbable plot.

First, at the beginning of the novel, all the principal characters are alone. Frances is divorced and her four children are rapidly growing to an age when they will no longer be dependent on her or living at home (RG, p. 203). She is estranged from her lover, Karel Schmidt, and her immediate family is "hardly a close-knit one" (RG, p. 12). When she is asked "to fill in her next of kin on her travel and insurance form", she doesn't know "whose name to put" (RG, p. 263).

She thinks of Karel as "the only man in Europe" (RG, p. 10). The phrase is descriptive as well as complimentary, since Karel's family "had perished in concentration camps. He alone of his generation had escaped" (RG, p. 23). Frances's brother Hugh is isolated by alcohol ("He drank at least half a bottle of scotch [every night], and if there was anything to celebrate he drank more" [RG,

p. 183]). One of her cousins, David Ollerenshaw, has "no wife, no brothers, no sisters, no children" and his contact with his "aging parents" is "almost nonexistent" (RG, p. 136). As for another, Janet Ollerenshaw Bird, housewife, "often she didn't speak to anyone all day except the baby and the people in the shops" (RG, p. 123). And it is months after her great-aunt Constance Ollerenshaw's death that a neighbour discovers her body.

   Second, there are an amazing number of scientists in this novel. Frances is an archaeologist. Her father is a biologist, her mother a gynecologist, her cousin a geologist whose father is a high school science teacher. Her lover is a historian (a social scientist). Janet Bird's husband is a chemical engineer. These sciences and scientists can be categorized according to their attitudes towards the past and towards life. Mark Bird, for instance, is a futuristic technologist, who is attempting to improve on nature by inventing "new kinds of indestructible matter" (RG, p. 156). His idea of conservation is to agitate for the preservation of the town gravel pit as a children's playground. Lady Ollerenshaw is an ardent crusader for birth control and abortion law reform ("she wanted more abortion, not less" [RG, p. 78]). Her husband, on the other hand, is a professor of zoology, a specialist on newts, which seem to Frances "survivors from a world of prehistory, born before the Romans arrived, before the bits of bronze-age pot sank in the swamp, remembering in their tiny bones the great bones of the stenosaurus, a symbol of God's undying contract with the earth" (RG, p. 104). David thinks of his uncle as "a brave man, to have mastered the dissection of newts". He prefers the inorganic because it is "pure" (RG, p. 335), but his reverence for rocks leads him to speculations that "in another age . . . might have been called religious":

> He saw order in the universe, he traced it along faults and folds, knowing that it was only ignorance that concealed the pattern, that the next outcrop existed surely, if only one could find it, and he had abandoned happily, indeed had never had (being born too late) the slightest sense of man as a necessary part of creation, as in any way a significant part. Man's life, as the Bible says, is grass, a mere breath: so was the whole history of mankind. This did not perturb him at all: on the contrary, he found the idea reassuring, for what he knew of man did not justify his taking of any very dignified part in the scale of creation (RG, p. 179).

Like Sir Frank, then, David reveres life. As a geologist, he simply takes a more comprehensive view of it. Also, as a geologist, "he [takes] a long view of time: even longer than Frances Wingate, archaeologist, and very much longer than Karel Schmidt, historian" (RG, p. 180).

Karel's speciality is the history of agriculture in eighteenth century England; Frances's the nomadic Phoenician traders of the Sahara. Frances hates the word "dig", because she does not think of her excavations as acts of violation: "she had not even pillaged the dead, on the contrary she had made them live again, and she had loved them, with their caravans and their date palms, their peaceful negotiations" (RG, p. 29). So too does Karel make the past live again, and perhaps for the same reason. For he admires the poetry of John Clare who "deplored the loss of the commons and the death of moles, in his great tenderness for the creation" (RG, p. 120).

These two observations – that the characters of *The Realms of Gold* are isolated from each other and that many of them are scientists, with various attitudes towards the past and towards life – can be related by way of Frances's question, "why had she become an archaeologist?" The answer, she decides, is that "the pursuit of archaeology . . . like the pursuit of history, is for such as myself and Karel [an] attempt to prove the possibility of the future through the past. We seek a utopia in the past, a possible if not an ideal society. We seek golden worlds from which we are banished . . ." (RG, pp. 120–121). Karel Schmidt, son of a Jewish doctor and a Polish journalist who perished in a concentration camp, looks to the past for evidence of life-supporting, life-enhancing networks of human relationship. So does Frances Wingate, who likes a book written by a colleague in anthropology because "it had argued a case for returning to Malinowski's simplistic theories about family ties" (RG, p. 231).

Frances's archaeological activity in this book is conducted not in the Sahara but in the English Midlands. There, excavating her family history, Frances makes a discovery more stupendous than the one which brought her renown as an archaeologist. She discovers in the past something that makes the future possible, not only for herself but for those whose attitudes allow them to share her vision. For some of its characters, at least, *The Realms of Gold* holds out the promise of an end to isolation through the establishment of new bonds of kinship.

2

Frances Wingate is at the centre of *The Realms of Gold* because she feels and articulates the malaise which characterizes the world she and the other characters inhabit. "I've got this terrible stone in my chest," she tells her brother (RG, p. 197). Perhaps it's boredom, she thinks at one point (RG, p. 221), but in fact it's loneliness. Dining by herself, missing Karel, Frances thinks desperately, "there must surely still be something in store. Hope springs eternal . . . But it was not hope that seemed to be springing and flourishing in her spiritual breast, it was a malignant and meaningless growth of grief. She felt as though she had swallowed a stone" (RG, p. 13). When the stone in her chest surfaces as a lump on her breast, it turns out to be not only benign, but benignant, since "in her illness [Frances] found herself turning rather weakly to her family. There was nowhere else to turn. She had no real friends, only colleagues and acquaintances, and she'd lost a lot of those during her years with Karel . . . She would have to come to terms with the future. She would have to make new connections" (RG, p. 77).

Forced by her brush with death to come to terms with her existential isolation, Frances turns with increasing zeal to her family, seeking to reactivate the web of kinship in which the individual has meaning and worth in relationship to others. While her first steps towards breaking out of her isolation involve visits to her parents and her brother, her more important task is to situate herself in a line of descent. Who are my ancestors and what have they bequeathed me, that I may pass on to my children? These are the questions that Frances begins to ask.

At first it seems to her that all she has been bequeathed is a disease, which she fears to pass on to her children. The Ollerenshaws' family history is "far from cheerful" (RG, p. 98). Looking back, Frances finds "melancholics [her father] and suicides [her sister]" and in the present generation "nomads [David], alcoholics [Hugh], and archaeologists [herself], with death running in their veins". Although she sometimes dignifies it with the name of Despair (RG, p. 6), Frances clearly believes that her family's hereditary disease is depression. And until the action of the novel begins, Frances has been fairly successful at warding it off:

> She had learned to deal with it by ignoring it, by denying its significance: she had refused to take it too seriously, but had it

sweat itself out like a dose of malaria. She had clung to activity
and movement as an escape, and on the whole her remedy had
worked: she had been able to evade the effects of the sickness, if
not the sickness itself (RG, p. 97).

But all Frances is doing, as she realizes, is masking symptoms. "Was
this all she was doing", she wonders, "feverishly seeking health by
trying to avoid illness? And what of her convictions, when in the
illness, that the illness had some deep spiritual significance?" (RG,
p. 97).

The significance of the Ollerenshaws' family disease may be that
it is not endemic but epidemic. Despair sickens everyone not only in
Frances's family but in this novel and, it might be argued, in this
society. Like Frances, most people ignore or deny the grievous fact
of their existential aloneness by frantic activity. Few have the
courage to confront it, as Frances finally does.

Recuperating from her operation, Frances acknowledges her
grief at being alone, the stone in her chest which will not go away. In
an attempt to "find out what it was that was worrying her" (RG,
p. 99), she resolves to visit Tockley, the Midlands town which is the
ancestral home of the Ollerenshaws.

Her visit to Tockley leaves Frances, if anything, even more
depressed. Her grandparents are dead, other people are living in
their cottage, and her favourite rural haunt has fallen victim to
industrial blight. So Frances returns to the anodyne of work and
accepts an invitation to attend an international conference on
developing nations in Adra.

But she carries the stone in her chest with her and it is in Adra that
her true return to Tockley begins. Joe Ayida, Adra's Minister of
Culture, is an art historian who is excited about Frances's Saharan
discoveries because he is interested in recovering Black history. "He
had talked a great deal about the history of Africa, and had been not
at all annoying on the subject: through him, she had glimpsed what
it must be like to have lost one's past, and to stand on the verge of
reclaiming it. The Greeks, the Romans, the Egyptians, he had said,
they have blinded us for centuries. She agreed" (RG, p. 222). Well
she might. It is not surprising that Frances should be sympathetic to
Joe Ayida's eagerness to uncover Black history from the cover-up
perpetrated by the Greeks, the Romans, the Egyptians. Frances too
has a history hidden from her by her father. According to him, the
present Ollerenshaws trace their descent from two cousins, Ted and

Enoch, who quarrelled at an early age and were never reconciled, thus accounting for Frances's ignorance of her cousins' existence: Frances comes from the line of Ted, Janet and David from the house of Enoch.

What Frances's father has never more than vaguely alluded to is the fact that Ted had a sister. While Frances is in Adra, becoming acquainted with her distant cousin, David, their mutual great-aunt dies, and by her death enables Frances to establish a new kinship network, kinship traced through the mothers, rather than the fathers.[2]

3

Adrienne Rich thinks that daughters naturally turn to their mothers for "mutual confirmation from and with another woman".[3] Neither Frances nor her sister Alice received this confirmation from their mother, a gynecologist who campaigns for population control and "more abortion, not less", a woman who doesn't "care much for sex", although "she like[s] sexual attention, and demand[s] it from the men around her" (RG, pp. 78–79). "Frigidity and gynecology", Frances thinks, are "a deadly combination" (RG, p. 81) which may have killed her sister, who committed suicide, Frances semi-seriously believes, in deference to her mother's passion for population control, "to reduce the family average". "She might have made the remark [aloud] had she not feared that her mother would not mind it. She is a woman without real affections, said Frances to herself" (RG, p. 81). Quite acutely, she observes that "although in theory a feminist, speaking frequently of the need to emancipate woman from the chores of domesticity and child-rearing, [her mother] seemed not to like other women". Not even her daughters.

"Matrophobia is the fear not of one's mother or of motherhood but of *becoming one's mother*",[4] and Frances spends her adolescence trying to deny that she is her mother's daughter: "she had pursued sex with determination rather than pleasure, resolving that what-ever she turned out like at least she wouldn't be like her mother" (RG, p. 81). Frances does not want to become her mother because she correctly identifies Lady Ollerenshaw as an unmotherly woman. This makes Frances, in effect, a motherless child. And "the woman who has felt 'unmothered' may seek mothers all her life".[5]

   This is what Frances finds when she returns to Tockley to arrange
her great-aunt's funeral. In Constance Ollerenshaw's cottage,
Frances reenacts a scene from an earlier Drabble novel. It may be
no accident that *The Realms of Gold* echoes the title of *Jerusalem the
Golden*. Both novels are about coming home and discovering one's
mother. When Clara Maugham returns to Northam to visit her
mother in the hospital, she discovers a cache of pictures and
notebooks that reveal her mother as a young woman, with dreams
and longings not very different from Clara's. Looking at them, Clara
feels kinship with her mother, feels "for the first time, the satisfaction
of her true descent". For the first *and* the last, since she does not act
on this emotion and subsequently represses it. When Frances
Wingate opens Constance Ollerenshaw's desk, she too finds "records going back into the dim reaches of the dusty Ollerenshaw
past . . . Nearly as indecipherable as hieroglyphics, nearly as sparse
in their information as Phoenician shopping lists, they contained a
past, a history" (RG, p. 299). What Frances discovers are pictures of
Constance as a young woman, proving – as Mrs. Maugham's old
photographs had to Clara – "that she had been a handsome girl".
She discovers school certificates, love letters, and the secret of Aunt
Con's reclusiveness: "a birth certificate for a daughter born to
Constance Ollerenshaw, June 15, 1914, in a nursing home in
Lincoln: a death certificate for the same child, who had died
eighteen months later" (RG, p. 301). She discovers that the child's
father had been married and had died young, leaving a widow and
two children. And she thinks that she too has a lover, who is married
to another woman, with whom he has had children.
"Frances . . . thought of Karel, as she read of Constance", and
then discovers that "she felt curiously at home, and private, feeding
twigs into her own hearth. Perhaps she herself would live here,
taking over where Con had left off" (RG, pp. 302–303). Identifying
with Constance, she finds at last "the satisfaction of her true
descent", as the lawyer who comes to fetch her unwittingly
acknowledges. Opening the door of the cottage, Harold Barnard
starts: "You could have been Constance herself, fifty years
younger", he says to Frances. "In this light" (RG, p. 304).
   Frances does buy Mays Cottage and finds there "a secure and all-
excluding secluded conclusion" to her search for an end to isolation,
with Karel and their two sets of children. "When asked where her
country cottage was, Frances would say, 'Near Tockley,' and
people would look at her as though she were mad, and she would

laugh, and say, it may not be paradise, but it suits me." To herself, she adds, "it was not quite as spectacular a rediscovery and reclamation as Tizouk, but it offered many private satisfactions" (RG, p. 352).

Among these are her discovery of a mother-figure who "confirms" her, who "illuminate[s] and expand[s] her sense of actual possibilities".[6] "The quality of the mother's life," Adrienne Rich writes, "is her primary bequest to her daughter, because a woman who can believe in herself, who is a fighter, and who continues to struggle to create livable space around her, is demonstrating to her daughter that these possibilities exist".[7] In identifying with Constance Ollerenshaw, Frances does not seek to emulate the details of her life – they were tragic – but its quality. Suffering "lost love, rejection, puerperal fever, guilt, interfering vicars, the death of a loved child, persecution by parents" (RG, p. 302), Connie nevertheless succeeded in creating livable space for herself. Rejecting patriarchy, which insists that women marry, raise children, and become consumers, Connie lived by herself and ate roots, berries, and snails. "And why not?" Frances asks. "Constance Ollerenshaw had lived simply and madly" (RG, p. 296), at harmony with herself and with nature. People called her a witch, and perhaps she was.

It may be, as Robin Morgan believes, that the history of witches is "part of [women's] entombed history, a remnant of the Old Religion [Wicce] which pre-dated all patriarchal faiths and which was a Goddess-worshipping, matriarchal faith".[8] It is certainly true that witches were regarded in sixteenth and seventeenth century Europe as "a socially indigestible group", intolerable to patriarchal culture, which burned them by the millions. As Mary Daly points out, "the witchcraze focused predominantly upon women who had rejected marriage (spinsters) and women who had survived it (widows)". And "lest there be any doubt that the motive of the European witchcraze was to purify society", Daly quotes the eminent scholar of witch hunting, H. D. Erik Midelfort:

Turning briefly to the larger social question of function, we can concede that the small trials may indeed have served a function, delineating the social thresholds of eccentricity tolerable to society, and registering fear of a socially indigestible group, unmarried women. . . . Until single women found a more comfortable place in the concepts and communities of Western men, one could argue that they were a socially disruptive element, at least when they lived without family and without patriarchal control. In this restricted sense the small witch trial may have even been therapeutic, or functional.[9]

The "prime target" of the witch hunters, Daly concludes, were "women who presented an option" to patriarchy.

Frances Wingate resents being called home from Adra to deal with her great-aunt's death because it prevents her from taking part in an archaeological dig which particularly attracts her. Preliminary excavation has uncovered, in a tin mine, a figurine "of a quite unexpected character" (RG, p. 256). "Quite unlike anything, it was, with its naturalistic features . . . and its stringy ropes of hair, all carved in terra cotta in a style no one had ever seen before. It had a witchy, androgynous, yet friendly look" (RG, p. 263) to Frances, who feels a "strong and sudden attraction" to it (RG, p. 256).

It is not surprising, then, that she should respond to the call of the witch in Constance Ollerenshaw, who "had expressed a request, in her will, that she should be buried in unconsecrated ground" (RG, p. 292). Her first impression of Connie's cottage (on "Hag's Lane, Barton-by-Tockley") is that it gives off an air of "terrible purity. . . . [and] she bowed her head in respect" to the woman "who had lived here alone for so long, whose death had been so solitary, so unremarked" (RG, p. 296).

Frances never knew her great-aunt. Few people did, so reclusive was her life. But Janet Bird has visited her, and she has therefore had a more vivid impression than Frances of Connie's witchy attraction. "She certainly looked like a witch", or rather like the Halloween caricature of a witch: "her hair was white, her nose was hooked, and she shook her fist at Janet and the pram". But Janet is not a little boy, to run away at the sight of a witch. Instead there is "something in her that loved the place" where Connie lives. "It was fierce and lonely", like Connie herself: "it was defiant. She liked it" (RG, p. 281). But she is too timid to speak to the witch. Instead, she leaves a box of chocolates on the window sill, as a way of "placat[ing] an ancient spirit, a spirit of blood" (RG, p. 282).

In identifying with Connie, Frances becomes something of a witch herself. Harold Barnard, who thinks she resembles her great-aunt as she sits by the fire, notes that "she had a curious look, crouched there in the firelight, her blond hair bleached but lit with red, her arms folded around her knees, shapeless in her large green jersey" (RG, pp. 305–306).

When Janet Bird finally meets Frances, she recognizes more profoundly than Harold Barnard Frances's witchiness. For what she sees is not the Halloween witch, but an independent woman, centred in her self, not controlled, as Janet feels herself to be, by patriarchy.

What Constance Ollerenshaw has confirmed in Frances is her power. As a strong, competent, professional woman, Frances is at home in a comradely relationship with her male colleagues (RG, p. 36). She regards her husband as an expendable stud (RG, p. 153) and presides efficiently over a husbandless household. In fact she decides that there's "no need for a man" and finds the nuclear family "unthinkable" (RG, pp. 233–234). Her brother sees her "not a captive" of male-dominated institutions, "but a queen", and tells her she looks exactly like Boadicea. "Thank you", she says. "I've been modeling myself on Boadicea for years" (RG, p. 201). Even her liaison with Karel is unconventional, by patriarchal standards. Himself an orphan, he moves into her house, bringing his children for her to raise. He even gives up his patrimony, his Middle European Jewish heritage, in taking refuge in "rural England", a haven he associates with Frances (RG, p. 334). When Connie dies, Sir Frank Ollerenshaw hands over the burial arrangements to his daughter, who sees herself as "the matriarch, arranging funerals. It was a role that she might have expected" (RG, p. 288).

There is no anthropological evidence that matriarchies – societies in which women have power over men – ever existed. "The golden age of woman is a myth".[10] But Michelle Zimbalist Rosaldo and Louise Lamphere argue that it is "a useful myth, a guide for present action, and that it is important insofar as it enjoins us to imagine a world in which women have real power . . . As a myth or a utopian vision, the idea of matriarchy has currency today as a source of hope for women".[11]

When Janet Bird looks at Frances Wingate, she has a vision of power – the power of being one's self. It is the same power she responded to in Constance Ollerenshaw. She and Frances almost immediately begin to talk, as mothers will, about their children, and Frances says that children do – and must – become "themselves" as they grow older. "I know what you mean", Janet says, "but I just don't see how it happens . . . I mean, I feel I am myself, and that I've got to look after it. But I don't know what it is. I know it's there,

that's all. That's why I don't think it was at all awful about Aunt
Con, she was being herself" (RG, p. 320). And then she makes the
connection between Aunt Con and Frances: "And as for you, it's
easy for you to know who you are . . . I can tell from looking at you,
who you are" (RG, p. 321).

Frances thinks that her restoration of Aunt Con's cottage, her
living there, has "offered many private satisfactions". But her
satisfaction extends at least to one other person:

> Having the cottage meant that [Frances] could keep in touch
> with Janet, which pleased them both. . . . [Frances] tried a little
> subversion on Janet, but wasn't very successful. Janet remained
> self-contained, dry, only intermittently communicative: she
> wasn't prepared to discuss her marriage with anybody. . . . But
> she liked to see Frances. It made a change to see Frances.
> Gradually, Janet came to believe that instead of confronting a life
> of boredom, she was merely biding her time (RG, pp. 352–353).

If Frances has been "strengthened and energized" by her discovery
of her "nonbiological mother", Constance Ollerenshaw, Janet Bird
finds strength in discovering, in Frances, her "spirit-sister".[12]

4

When Frances returns to Tockley, her personal quest for a mother
merges with the larger theme introduced by the octopus in his
plastic box. "Matter and mother are etymologically connected",
Mary Daly reminds us,[13] and Adrienne Rich elaborates: "The
words for mother and mud (earth, slime, the matter of which the
planet is composed, the dust or clay of which 'man' is built) are
extremely close in many languages: *mutter, madre, mater, materia,
moeder, modder*".[14]

"One of the fundamental theoretical contributions of the
women's movement", Anne Barstow writes, "has been to point out
the ways in which women have been identified with what is bodily,
procreative, and finite; while men have claimed the attributes of
reason, creativity, and transcendence".[15] And Sherry B. Ortner
tells us that culture is "still equated relatively unambiguously with
men", while women are thought to have "more direct affinity with
nature". Moreover, "culture . . . at some level of awareness asserts

itself to be not only distinct from but superior to nature, and that sense of distinctiveness and superiority rests precisely on the ability to transform – to 'socialize' and 'culturalize' – nature".[16] Science and technology define nature as "the Other", to be tamed, domesticated, exploited, and occasionally raped. Rosemary Ruether sees as the inevitable denouement of this dualistic patriarchal thinking "ecological disaster".[17]

So does David Ollerenshaw, who fears what may happen should man "take into his own hands the destruction of matter itself". What *is* happening, in our technological society, is that man is destroying matter in order to replace it with the kind of plastics Mark Bird is developing – "new kinds of indestructible matter".

When Frances was a child, her grandparents' cottage in Tockley had seemed "like paradise, like the original garden" (RG, p. 102). Her favourite place had been a ditch behind the cottage. "Canadian pondweed grew in the water: purplespikes and poppies and ragwort and teasels grew on the banks. In the spring there were celandines and cowslips . . . There were water boatmen, large beetles, tadpoles, frogs, minnows, stickleback, grubs, caddis larvae, water rats, newts, a whole unnecessary and teeming world of creation" (RG, p. 103). Returning as an adult, she discovers that "a thick oily scum [now] covered the water: bits of paper, fag ends, Coca-Cola bottles, an old tire, a chunk of polystyrene, and a car seat floated in it" (RG, p. 115). The primal fecundity of the ditch has been fouled by the unnatural, anti-natural detritus of industrialization and technology.

Remembering this ditch, Frances arrives at Constance Ollerenshaw's cottage expecting to find "decay, rusty, corrugated iron, tin cans, broken bottles, rotten planks, dung heaps, the worst . . . But instead there was a cottage, overgrown with thorns and brambles, crumbling and falling, but crumbling to nature only, not to man . . . The cottage felt all right. It even had a feeling of home. It was contained, it was secret . . . Nature had gently enfolded it, had embraced it and taken it and thicketed it in, with many thorns and briars; nature had wanted it, and had not rejected it" (RG, pp. 296, 299).

Mary Daly redeems the radical meaning of the word "gynecology" by slashing it with a virgule so that its etymological components will be seen in their correct relationship. Far from being, as Webster and Lady Ollerenshaw define it, "the branch of medicine dealing with the study and treatment of women's diseases", gyn/ecology is the "science" of women's discovering "the complex web of interrelationships between organisms and their environment . . . In contrast to gynecology, which depends upon fixation and dismemberment, Gyn/Ecology affirms that everything is connected".[18] To the extent that Frances's search for a mother returns her to nature, the "maternal matrix of being",[19] *The Realms of Gold* is a "gyn/ecological" book.[20]

5

At the beginning of *The Realms of Gold*, Frances Wingate is a motherless child, alienated from her lover and her children, alone in an insulated, air-conditioned hotel room. At the end of the novel, she is living in Mays Cottage with Karel and their two sets of children, literally cultivating her garden. Discovering her spiritual mother has reoriented Frances. No longer depressed or despairing, she is "overcome with joy" (RG, p. 350). Margaret Drabble has said that novels by women can serve women as blueprints. So it is fair to ask how usable France's story is as a paradigm for women. Does it teach us how to correct that "spiritual imbalance" David Ollerenshaw detects in modern technological society in which men have "elevated spirit against matter"? At least one reviewer thinks it may. "I have tried to do little more than lay out this novel in a celebrating way", Roger Sale writes, "because I believe it, every word. The joy at the end overwhelms disbelief". Yet his concluding sentence reveals the wish-fulfilling nature of his confidence. Drabble has created, he writes, "the private history of an England that, if only in this beautiful novel, is becoming a realm of gold".[21]

The Realms of Gold is a beautiful novel. But despite its happy ending, it is not, finally, very optimistic about the condition of England and of contemporary society. France's "satisfactions", her "joy", are merely private. However inspiring she may be to Janet Bird, she is helpless to prevent the suicide of her nephew, who more than any other character in the novel symbolizes modern, alienated man. Karel tries to console Frances by pointing out that "she had clearly represented for [Stephen] one of the only possible patterns of living" (RG, p. 347), and Stephen's suicide note suggests that Karel is right: "Don't think I haven't loved you, Aunt Frances . . . don't think I haven't been impressed by your approach. I have. But it's not for me" (RG, p. 345). Earlier in the novel, Stephen questions

Frances about her energy and her optimism, but when she tries to explain her philosophy he can only "gaze at her in wonder, as though she belonged to another species, as though she were an angel floating in the upper reaches of meaningless heavenly activity, as though she were a bird or a fish" (RG, p. 86). Stephen's "problems [are] not personal" (RG, p. 204); he suffers simply for being sensitive enough to experience the despair we all feel when we look at the mess man has made of our world. Frances's "approach" to life is potentially revolutionary. By aligning herself with the mothers, by returning to nature, she is at least diagnosing the ills of contemporary society and naming their cause, patriarchy and patriarchal thinking. But her solution is personal rather than political.

More disturbingly, since *The Waterfall* and *The Needle's Eye* had conceded that the personal can do no more than "verge" on the political and that perhaps the only way to fight patriarchy is to live invisibly if subversively on the boundaries of its institutions, the narrative method of *The Realms of Gold* suggests that even such private satisfactions as Frances finds may be hard to come by. In her afterword to Monica Mannheimer's article on *The Needle's Eye*, Drabble makes this comment: "In the novel which I have just finished, *The Realms of Gold*, the characters do indeed appear to behave with much more freedom and spontaneity [than Rose and Simon] . . . But this appearance of freedom and happiness can only be achieved by a lot of tricks in the plot . . ." As in *The Needle's Eye*, Drabble chooses omniscience as her narrative mode in *The Realms of Gold*. But the unobtrusiveness of the convention in *The Needle's Eye* is replaced in this novel by a noisy declaration of authorial presence. I count some 35 authorial intrusions in *The Realms of Gold*. Some are brief (David "rubbed his glasses on his handkerchief. Remember him, for it will be some months before he and Frances Wingate meet again" [RG, p. 51]). Some go on for paragraphs (see, for instance, pages 152, 169, 180–181, and the last five pages of the novel, in which the narrator tells us what happens to the major characters after the action of the novel ends). All of them emphasize the point made at the conclusion of this passage:

> The picture postcard which Frances Wingate had written to [Karel Schmidt] at the beginning of the year was at that moment lifted from its resting place at the bottom of a mail bag a thousand miles away, and sent upon its way. Its journey from box to bag had taken nine months: the rest of its journey was to take a mere

ten days. And to those who object to too much coincidence in fiction, perhaps one could point out that there is very little real coincidence in the postcard motif, though there are many other coincidences in this book (RG, p. 218).

Indeed there are: that Frances and David should meet in Africa, that Karel and David should miss a plane that crashes in the English Channel, that Karel's wife should discover she's a lesbian just when Karel and Frances want to get married. Even minor details are coincidental. In Tockley, Frances makes two phone calls – to the vicar and to Janet Bird. The vicar is eating his supper when she calls. "Janet Bird was also eating her supper when Frances Wingate rang. The vicar had been eating shepherd's pie, cauliflower, and frozen peas. Janet Bird was eating shepherd's pie and frozen peas too, though she had no cauliflower. There is some limit to life's coincidences" (RG, p. 311).

But there is no limit to the coincidences which provide this novel's happy ending. And the most fortuitous of all is the one the narrator underplays, the postcard motif. Had it not been for the accident of a postal strike, Karel would have received Frances's summons to return to her days, rather than months, after she mailed it. And since "he had always promised that, if asked, he would return" (RG, p. 42), she would have been saved the necessity and denied the opportunity of discovering her maternal roots.

"In *The Needle's Eye*, I made life as difficult as possible for the characters; in *The Realms of Gold* I made it as easy as possible. The truth probably lies half way between, as far as probability goes"[22] I don't think Margaret Drabble believes that. I think she believes that *The Needle's Eye* is essentially true and that *The Realms of Gold* is not only a work of fiction but fictitious. "I have never had very high expectations of happiness", she has said. Why then would she want us to take the happy ending of *The Realms of Gold* seriously? In fact, she won't let us, and readers who nominate *The Realms of Gold* as their favourite Drabble novel because of its optimism are simply not listening to its author/narrator when she insists on the arbitrariness of the happy ending:

[Frances] tidied the cottage up, gradually: on the first few visits, she managed to get there alone with Karel, and they slept together among the cobwebs, making good lost months and years, in a terrifying, a safe, a giddy, a precarious, a secure and all-excluding secluded conclusion, as final in its own way as Stephen's had been: as final, as ruthless, and, it seemed, as natural. Resent it, if you like. She will not care: she is not listening. A happy ending, you may say (RG, p. 352).

This brief passage can produce vertigo in the attentive reader. Frances's and Karel's seclusion is safe and secure, from one point of view, and terrifying, giddy, precarious, and ruthless, from another. This "happy" ending "seems" as "natural" as Stephen's nihilistic suicide; the reader is tacitly being invited to take her pick. And further to disconcert the reader, we are reminded that Frances is not a real person who may conceivably serve as a model for us: "she is not listening", or more accurately, she cannot hear, because we are on one side of the printed page and she is on the other.

Anthea Zeman calls *The Realms of Gold* "a defiantly, blatantly optimistic novel from a professed pessimist".[23] It is an aberration. The age of gold is succeeded by *The Ice Age*.

NOTES

[1] Margaret Drabble, *The Realms of Gold* (New York: Alfred A. Knopf, 1975), p. 3. Further references to RG will appear in the text.

[2] I was heartened to discover corroboration of the kind of analysis I undertake in the following section in a paper delivered by Carey Kaplan at the Women and Society Symposium held at St. Michael's College, Winooski, Vermont, in March of 1979. In "A Vision of Power in Margaret Drabble's *The Realms of Gold*", Kaplan traces a pattern of "extravagantly uterine imagery" in the novel and shows that it becomes a metaphor of "the powerful establishment of harmony and integration". This uterine imagery, she argues, "almost inevitably considers the organic relationship of the present to the past and the future". It is, she concludes, "an imagery of immense creative power". I agree wholeheartedly and am grateful to Carey Kaplan for allowing me to read and quote from her as yet unpublished paper.

[3] Adrienne Rich, *Of Woman Born: Motherhood as Experience and Institution* (New York: Bantam Books, 1977), p. 213.

[4] Ibid., p. 237.

[5] Ibid., p. 245.

[6] Ibid., p. 250.

[7] Ibid., pp. 250–251.

[8] Robin Morgan, *Going Too Far: The Personal Chronicle of a Feminist* (New York: Random House, 1977), p. 71.

[9] H. C. Erik Midelfort, *Witch Hunting in Southwestern Germany, 1562–1684: The Social and Intellectual Foundations* (Stanford: Stanford University Press, 1972), p. 3. As quoted in *Gyn/Ecology*, op. cit., p. 184.

[10] Simone de Beauvoir, TSS, p. 64. This opinion is shared by most modern anthropologists. See Michelle Zimbalist Rosaldo and Louise Lamphere, eds., *Woman, Culture, and Society* (Stanford: Stanford University Press, 1974), Ernestine Friedl, *Women and Men: An Anthropologist's View* (New York: Holt, Rinehart, and Winston, 1975), and Paula Webster, "Matriarchy: A Vision of Power", in *Toward an Anthropology of Women*, ed. Rayna R. Reiter (New York and London: Monthly Review Press, 1975).

[11] Rosaldo and Lamphere, op. cit., from the editors' introduction, p. 4.

[12] These terms are Adrienne Rich's and Mary Daly's. See Rich, op. cit., p. 257.

[13] *Gyn/Ecology*, p. 218.

[14] Rich, op. cit., p. 96.

[15] Anne Barstow, "The Uses of Archaeology for Women's History: James Mellaart's Work on the Neolithic Goddess at Catal Huyuk", *Feminist Studies*, Vol. 4, No. 3 (October 1978), 10.

[16] Sherry B. Ortner, "Is Female to Male as Nature is to Culture?" in Rosaldo and Lamphere, op. cit., p. 73.

[17] Rosemary Radford Ruether, *New Woman/New Earth: Sexist Ideologies and Human Liberation* (New York: Seabury Press, 1975), p. 194.

[18] *Gyn/Ecology*, pp. 9, 11.

[19] *New Woman/New Earth*, p. 194.

[20] It cannot be accidental that Frances's unmotherly mother (who does not really care for women) is a gynecologist. Gynecology is the science in which the equation of matter and mother is clearest; it is a profession – dominated by men – which seeks to dominate women and nature, or natural functions. As Adrienne Rich painfully records, modern gynecology and obstetrics developed in the nineteenth century, when midwives' "hands of flesh" were ruthlessly supplanted by "hands of iron", forceps wielded by male obstetricians who decided when and how women would give birth. See Rich, op. cit., chapters six and seven.

[21] Roger Sale, "The Realms of God", *Hudson Review*, Vol. 28, No. 4 (Winter 1975–76), 628.

[22] "The Author Comments", op. cit.

[23] Anthea Zeman, *Presumptuous Girls: Women and Their World in the Serious Woman's Novel* (London: Weidenfeld and Nicolson, 1977), p. 150.

6 "Fed up with women": *The Ice Age*

"What do you find most difficult in writing your novels?" someone recently asked Margaret Drabble. "I find it very difficult to write about very stupid people", she answered. "And men. Writing about men".[1] Drabble's fictional world is populated by women who are "not only intelligent, but intelligent about themselves",[2] and by men who – when they are not absent, like Sarah Bennett's boyfriend – are negligible stock characters. Not until *The Needle's Eye* did Drabble create, in Simon Camish, a believably human male character. And Simon is in many ways a woman-identified man. His attention, like the reader's, is focused on Rose Vassiliou and he is drawn sympathetically because he attempts to understand and appreciate the female point of view. David Ollerenshaw in *The Realms of Gold*, on the other hand, is a man's man. He has no wife, no mistress, no particular interest in women. And he is as enigmatic to Margaret Drabble as he is to Frances Wingate, who is inspired by contemplating David to observe that "human nature is truly impenetrable" (RG, p. 354). This is what Drabble has to say about him: "The truth is that David was intended to play a much larger role in this narrative, but the more I looked at him, the more incomprehensible he became . . ." (RG, p. 176).

But by the time she came to write *The Ice Age*, Drabble was "fed up with women".[3] So she makes her central protagonist a man, and discloses in her portrait of Anthony Keating that it is not so difficult for her to write about a man as she had thought. Her description of Anthony's lover, Alison Murray, for example, was written by a woman who – at least for the moment – sees her through a man's eyes:

> She was the kind of woman one could take anywhere. Merchant bankers treated her with respect. She was dark, with one of those pale, oval, sad, soft, expressive faces that are as typically English

as the English rose: refined, delicate, slightly but not uneasily withdrawn. Her large, expressive dark eyes had once looked into the hearts of those sitting in the back rows of the stalls [she has been an actress]: when they turned their gaze upon Anthony, upon a merchant banker, upon a rich benefactor, their appeal could hardly be resisted. And she had remarkable legs. The clean, thin line of shin and ankle, the precision, the articulation, were a joy to behold. . . . Her skin was also remarkable. It had a clear, pale, translucent smoothness, blue veins adorned her inner arm, her thighs, her breasts, her elegant neck.[4]

On the evidence of the earlier novels, one would have expected Drabble to focus on Alison Murray. And indeed she does move us into Alison's consciousness long enough to establish her awareness of how frail her power is in a man's world. Looking in a mirror, Alison sees signs of aging. "When will I cease to be able to look at myself naked in the mirror?" she asks. "And God, oh God, what then, what then will I do?" But although the narrator observes that, in a man's world, "for Alison Murray, beauty had for years been identity" and that "she had had no other" (IA, p. 94), Drabble's intention in *The Ice Age* does not seem primarily to be to condemn man's inhumanity to woman, but to take a serious look at masculine values. Hence she focuses not on Alison Murray nor on Maureen Kirby, the other principal woman in the novel, but on their lovers, Anthony Keating, Len Wincobank, Derek Ashby, and on a number of other men who, like David Ollerenshaw, are only marginally interested in women.

Anthony Keating and his associates are, he thinks, "at one with the spirit of the age" (IA, p. 30). Financiers, speculators, architects, city planners, property developers, they play games and take chances. They have power and they glory in its exercise, which takes the same form in this novel as it did in *The Realms of Gold*. For the central male enterprise in *The Ice Age* is the assertion of the superiority of culture over nature. In *The Realms of Gold* this attitude was indicted as leading to ecological disaster. But the point of view in that novel was female. Here, the male enterprise is viewed from a male perspective. For Len Wincobank, the cities of America represent the apex of man's achievement, the glorious demonstration of his creative energy:

He thought of America. New York, the most beautiful city in the world, the apotheosis of aspiration. What buildings there, what inspiration, what vision, what glory, steel, glass, concrete, Art Nouveau, Art Deco, Brutality, fountains, spires, windows, avenues, intersections, passion, and desire. Or Chicago, with the glittering lakefront, the water that flowed backward, the highest building in the world, a paradise of invention and felicity (IA, p. 49)[5]

The architect Derek Ashby, marvelling at Sheffield's new city centre, thinks he is "lucky to have been born in such a time, in such a city, when there was still energy, when men could still build views and windows" (IA, pp. 167–168). Len Wincobank knows that in the architecture of the future, there will be no need for windows. Who needs fresh air when man-made air conditioning can provide 70 degrees of perfectly humidified comfort at the touch of a button? Who needs a view when rooms can be carpeted wall to wall in "thick green . . . like grass" (IA, p. 84)?

In *The Realms of Gold*, Frances Wingate thought of Shelley and "the absolute futility of all human effort. My name is Ozymandias, King of Kings: Look on my works, ye Mighty, and despair!" (RG, p. 222). Anthony Keating interprets the sonnet differently. "Ozymandias, King of Kings. Look on my works, ye mighty. Well, he hadn't been far wrong, Ozymandias, he had lost his kingdom, perhaps, but at least part of his monument remained. By their monuments ye shall know them. By the Pyramids, the Parthenon, by Chartres and the Hancock Building, by St. Pancras Station and the Eiffel Tower, by the Post Office Tower and the World Trade Center. . . . Man's own achievement, they point to the skies" (IA, p. 200). Even stone walls are a sign of man's achievement. Anthony "liked the way they marched across the contours, and up the steep slopes. He liked their gray whitenesses, their persistence, their human scale, their mathematical parcelling out of the infinite. They squared it off and captured it . . ." (IA, p. 149). Anthony's own monument is an abandoned gas holding tank he has bought from the London Gas Board. Though "derelict", it is "radiant with significance" for Anthony: "It was painted a steely gray-blue, and it rose up against the sky like a part of the sky itself; iron air, a cloud, a mirage, a paradox, defining a space of sky. . . . It was a work of art" (IA, p. 27).

In *The Needle's Eye* and *The Realms of Gold*, Drabble subjected such patriarchal visions to feminist censure. And such censure is not wholly absent from *The Ice Age*. Where Anthony sees a work of art, Alison Murray sees "man-made dereliction", a "wasteland", something "monstrous, inhuman, ludicrous". The redeveloped city centre of Northam, one of Len Wincobank's pet projects, strikes Alison as "an environmental offense as bad as a slag heap" (IA, pp. 170–174). Similarly, although she admires her boyfriend's energy and enjoys his wealth, Maureen Kirby secretly criticizes Len Wincobank for being inhuman, for thinking of buildings and forgetting the people inside of them. Uncritically, Len himself looks at a new high-rise apartment building and thinks, "What did he care if the families in it went to the bad . . . what did it matter if they went mad like animals too constantly displayed in their cages in a zoo? The building was beautiful; it sang out" (IA, p. 47). Before he became a property developer himself, Anthony Keating accused Len Wincobank of "raping the city centres of Britain" (IA, p. 21). After his "conversion" (IA, p. 28) to Len's way of thinking, he "began to see even the Northam center with new eyes" (IA, p. 29).

The only eyes which continue to see Len Wincobank's projects clearsightedly are female. This should not surprise anyone who has read *The Realms of Gold*. In that novel, the superiority of culture over nature was asserted by science and technology. In this, culture manifests itself as art and architecture. But the dynamic is the same, one which Wallace Stevens discloses in one of his meditations on art:

> I placed a jar in Tennessee,
> And round it was, upon a hill.
> It made the slovenly wilderness
> Surround that hill.
>
> The wilderness rose up to it,
> And sprawled around, no longer wild.
> The jar was round upon the ground
> And tall and of a port in air.
>
> It took dominion everywhere . . .

Art – some would call it the highest manifestation of culture – is the imposition of order on chaos, the domination of nature, the victory of the male over the female principle. For who can fail to see that Stevens' jar is male, his wilderness female? Alison Murray, who does not share Anthony Keating's phallocentric vision, demands to know what "people like you have done to the face, to the very *face* of the country" (IA, p. 180).

Anthony hedges a bit, pointing out that "there have been some good buildings built" and mentioning the Clean Air Act and other recent environmental legislation. But when pressed, he is forced to admit that men have made a mess of things. London has become "unpleasant", he concedes. It is "going the way of New York – garbage-strewn, transport-choked, dirty, violent" (IA, p. 65). So he decides to "opt out" and move to the country (IA, p. 176). But Alison won't let him opt out of his responsibility for the mess things are in: "I do think it's a bit awful of you, Anthony, to knock other places down, and that nice Mr. Boot from the sweets factory, and drive them out, and put up all those great blocks, and then come and sit up her in this – this Ancient Monument, and say you like it. Of course you like it. But it just isn't consistent of you, is it?" (IA, p. 180). It is not only inconsistent but unfair that Anthony Keating should retire to a country estate with the money he has made rendering city centres uninhabitable. So when the bottom falls out of the market, when the boom turns to bust and Anthony loses his money, even "he could see the poetic justice of it" (IA, p. 9). And there is more than poetic justice operating in the verdict that sends Len Wincobank to jail for fraud.

Because the action of the novel occurs after the economic crash in which Anthony and his associates lost their fortunes, Alison's feminist critique of their erstwhile success is muted. Instead, another note is sounded. "These are terrible times we live in", a friend writes Anthony, and in a "state of the nation" interlude, the narrator expands this statement:

All over the nation, families who had listened to the news looked at one another and said, "Goddness me," or "Whatever next," or "I give up," or "Well, fuck that" . . . A huge icy fist, with large cold fingers, was squeezing and chilling the people of Britain, that great and puissant nation, slowing down their blood, locking them into immobility, fixing them in a solid stasis, like fish in a frozen river: there they all were in their large houses and their small houses, with their first mortgages and second mortgages, in their rented flats and council flats and basement bed-sits and their caravans: stuck, congealed, among possessions, in attitudes, in achievements they had hoped next month to shed, and with which they were now condemned to live. The flow had ceased to flow; the ball had stopped rolling; the game of musical chairs was over. *Rien ne va plus*, the croupier had shouted (IA, pp. 59–60).

The title, *The Ice Age*, Drabble explained to one reviewer, was "shorthand for economic depression – everything frozen including wages. But I don't want Americans to read *The Ice Age* as a portrait of England going down the drain".[6] As she says elsewhere, Drabble wanted in this novel "to put England's problems into some larger context".[7]

That larger context is philosophical. What makes these times terrible is not that wages are frozen. This situation can be explained and a remedy conceived. What is terrible – or more accurately, terrifying – is what cannot be explained.

Anthony can explain and accept as just his loss of money. But why, at 38, should he have had a heart attack? "Unexpected illnesses often strike their victims as punishments for known or unknown crimes", the narrator remarks (IA, p. 65), and Anthony tries to see his heart attack as punishment for hubris. But then he reflects that it was really his partner "who had suffered from hubris", and that therefore "it was Giles who ought to have had a heart attack. Anyway, physically, he was more the type: a fat man, a heavy man, a heavy drinker and a heavy smoker, a man who took no exercise of any sort". Whereas Anthony "had been extremely fit, light, energetic, if anything underweight, a walker and a squash player" (IA, p. 10).

Most of the terrible things that happen in this novel have nothing to do with economic depression. Kitty Friedmann, who observes that we live in terrible times, is writing from the hospital. She was maimed in "a ghastly, arbitrary accident" (IA, p. 6). She and her husband Max, a business associate of Anthony's, had been celebrating their ruby wedding anniversary in a London restaurant and a bomb, planted by the IRA, had exploded, taking Kitty's foot and Max's life. "I don't know what Max ever did to deserve it", Kitty thinks. Perhaps if the PLO had planted the bomb, there would have been at least poetic justice in Max's death, since he has "donated liberally to Israel". But "Max and Kitty had nothing whatsoever to do with the Irish" (IA, p. 6). "Why Kitty, why Max, why Anthony Keating? And why had the punishments been so unrelated to the offences?" (IA, p. 6).

The biggest injustice of all, as Dostoevsky knew, is the suffering of children. Alison Murray has two daughters. One is in jail and rightly so. The other, 10 year old Molly, is in a prison far more confining than her sister's and one which she did nothing to deserve. "Whatever happens to you", Alison tells Jane, "it can't be as bad as what happened before birth to Molly", who has cerebral palsy and a probable IQ of 60, just enough to give her "awareness, frustration, inexpressible understandings that could find no normal outlet" (IA, p. 143). Alison had devoted her life to Molly, and Anthony, contemplating the two of them, "the one so perfectly, so delicately articulated, the other so inarticulate in every way", asks, "What was it for? A joke, a trial, a punishment? Too much had been asked of Alison". What he sees when he looks at Alison and Molly is "a vision of irredeemable injustice" (IA, pp. 182–183).

The Ice Age is prefaced with two epigraphs, Wordsworth's "Milton! thou shouldst be living at this hour:/England hath need of thee . . ." and Milton's own impassioned apostrophe to his native land: "Methinks I see in my mind a noble and puissant Nation rousing herself like a strong man after sleep, and shaking her invincible locks . . ." It is the Milton of *Areopagitica* whom Wordsworth invokes and Drabble quotes, the Milton who exhorted his "noble and puissant Nation" to fulfill its birthright. But once invoked, Milton will not be harnessed to Wordsworth's intentions or Drabble's. Brooding over *The Ice Age* is the spirit of Milton, not the political polemicist, but the philosophical poet.

By the time he wrote *Paradise Lost* in 1667, Milton was prepared to "assert Eternal Providence,/And justify the ways of God to Men". In 1637 he had not been so sure that they were justifiable. When a Cambridge friend of the young Milton's was drowned in the Irish Sea, his classmates put together a group of elegies mourning his death. Milton's contribution was *Lycidas*, which records not so much his grief at the death of Edward King as his own spiritual crisis. For what King's death forced Milton to consider was the question of justice. Why should a gifted man die young? What had he done to deserve it?

Apparently nothing. So Milton is confronted with several ways of accounting for King's death. It was an accident, a demonstration that the universe is governed by no divine purpose or natural order. Chance, not the gods, determines human affairs:

> Where were ye Nymphs when the remorseless deep
> Clos'd o'er the head of your lov'd Lycidas?
> . . .

Ay me, I fondly dream!
Had ye been there – for what could that have done?
What could the Muse herself that Orpheus bore,
The Muse herself, for her enchanting son
Whom Universal nature did lament,
When by the rout that made the hideous roar,
His gory visage down the stream was sent,·
Down the swift Hebrus to the Lesbian shore?

Terrifying as that idea is, it is less awful to contemplate than
another. What if King's death was not, as Anthony Keating thinks
Max Friedmann's was, "a ghastly, arbitrary accident"? What if the
universe is governed not by chance but by fate? And what if that fate
be neither benevolent nor indifferent to man, but hostile? What if
Fate behaves like a Fury?

But the fair Guerdon when we hope to find,
And think to burst out into sudden blaze,
Comes the blind Fury with th'abhorred shears,
And slits the thin-spun life.

Looking around him, Milton can see no more evidence than any of
the characters in *The Ice Age* that there is anything like justice in the
world. And he draws the only reasonable conclusion. The universe
is governed either by chance or by a spirit hostile to man. These are
the alternative explanations offered by various characters in *The Ice
Age* for the terrible things that happen to apparently innocent
people. And although it is discomfiting to think events have no
meaning, it is terrifying to glimpse, as Alison Murray once does, "a
primitive causality so shocking, so uncanny, that she shivered and
froze. A world where the will was potent, not impotent: where it
made, indeed, bad choices and killed others by them, killed them,
deformed them, destroyed them" (IA, pp. 96–97). No, Alison
decides, "one must continue to behave as though one believed in the
accidental" (IA, p. 155) if one is to avoid existential terror. That is
the only reasonable way out of the philosophical dilemma posed by
Lycidas and reiterated by *The Ice Age*.

But Milton discovers another way out. Despite the evidence, he
concludes *Lycidas* with the flat assertion that there *is* a destiny that
shapes our ends and that, moreover, it is benevolent:

Weep no more, woeful Shepherds weep no more,
For Lycidas your sorrow is not dead,
Sunk though he be beneath the watry floor.
So sinks the day-star in the Ocean bed,
And yet anon repairs his drooping head,
And tricks his beams, and with new-spangled Ore,
Flames in the forehead of the morning sky:
So Lycidas, sunk low, but mounted high,
Through the dear might of him that walk'd the waves.

At the end of *Lycidas*, Milton makes the leap of faith, and employs the syntax of faith – paradox – to express his irrational conviction that God *is* in his heaven and all *is* right with the world.

At the end of *The Ice Age*, Anthony Keating is in a prison camp behind the iron curtain as a result of what he would have called earlier in the novel an arbitrary accident. Others might have blamed fate. But Anthony "cannot bring himself to believe in the random malice of the fates, those three gray sisters" (IA, p. 294), and he has apparently come round to Alison's view that "there is no such thing as an accident" (IA, p. 155). What is left, but to make the gratuitous leap of faith? "I do not know how man can do without God", Anthony says (IA, p. 265). "If God did not appoint this trial for me, then how could it be that I should be asked to endure it, he asks". Like the older Milton, "he is determined, alone, to justify the ways of God to man" (IA, p. 294).

When Alison writes Anthony, asking how to handle his affairs while he's in prison, he answers that "she should do what she wished . . . God would advise her". "This last sentence perplexed Alison extremely. God would advise her? Who was God? Was it a code name for Giles Peters or Len Wincobank?" (IA, p. 288). That may be the funniest line in the novel. It may also be the most serious.

At the beginning of *The Ice Age*, Anthony Keating is spiritually bankrupt. He has rejected the faith of his father, "a churchman and a schoolmaster" (IA, p. 14) and is therefore "ripe for conversion, to some new creed. A political creed, but there wasn't one; a religious creed, but he had had God, along with his father and life in the cathedral close. So what would happen to the vacant space in Anthony Keating? What would occupy it? The vacant space was occupied by Len Wincobank; the conversion took place in 1968 . . ." (IA, p. 21). Under Len's tutelage, Anthony comes to see more beauty and significance in a gasometer than in a cathedral

(IA, p. 27), yet he perceives their kinship. Both are symbols of "man's own achievement" (IA, p. 200).

So, from one point of view, is a religious creed. The edifice of faith is built upon paradox, just as Anthony's gasometer, with its "delicate, airy, elaborately simple" form is "a paradox." For the heroes of *Paradise Lost*, that paradox is grounded upon the certitude of God's providence, intermittently revealed in human affairs through divine intervention. When God orders Abraham to leave his home and go "into a land/Which he will show him", Abraham "straight obeys,/Not knowing to what land, yet firm believes". Though paradoxical, Abraham's faith is not quixotic. It is grounded in the revealed fact of God's existence and benevolence.

Anthony Keating does not read *Paradise Lost* in prison, but *The Consolation of Philosophy*, and "Anthony is interested in the fact that [Boethius] found consolation more in philosophy than in faith" (IA, p. 293). Written in 524, *The Consolation of Philosophy* became "a cornerstone of medieval humanism"[8] because, unlike patristic theology, it limits its consideration of the human condition "to the powers of natural reason without direct recourse, or even mention of, Christian revelation." Like Augustine before and Milton after him, Boethius "undertook to justify the ways of God to men, to explore philosophically the mysteries of the divine will as it is manifested in the order, and apparent disorder, of temporal events". In the form of a dialogue between the imprisoned Boethius and a personified Philosophy, *The Consolation* – like Anthony's gasometer – is a "delicate, airy, elaborately simple" *logical* construction, "proving" that although "you cannot discern the order that governs [events], nevertheless everything is governed by its own proper order directing all things toward the good" (Book 4, Prose 6). In the view of one recent translator, *The Consolation of Philosophy* is Boethius's "record of the victory of reason and hope over the despair brought on by personal disaster". It stands testimony to "the liberating power of the mind, the self-mastery which comes from a just estimate of the limited value of material, and therefore transitory, satisfactions".

From the female perspective, there is no consolation in Boethius's philosophy or Anthony's. The narrator leaves Anthony in prison, rejoicing at the sight of a bird he thinks may be "a messenger from God, an angel, a promise". Then she returns us to earth and to Alison. "Alison there is no leaving. Alison can neither live nor die. Alison has Molly. Her life is beyond imagining. It will not be imagined. Britain will recover, but not Alison Murray" (IA, p. 195).

Britain will recover because men like Anthony Keating will recover. A thoroughgoing feminist analysis of Anthony's religious conversion reveals that it is no conversion at all from the kind of thinking which produced the economic expansion and ecological crisis of the sixties. At the height of his prosperity, Anthony Keating sees himself as "a modern man, an operator, at one with the spirit of the age" (IA, p. 30). By the end of the novel, he thinks instead that he is an anachronism: "I might as well accept that I belong to the world that has gone, reared in the shelter of a cathedral built to a faith that I have sometimes wished I could share, educated in ideals of public service which I have sometimes wished I could fulfill, a child of a lost empire" (IA, pp. 259–260). From a feminist perspective, it is irrelevant that Anthony decide whether he is "a man of the past, the present, the future" (IA, p. 206). He is a man, and "he and his clever friends" who gamble with the stock market are no different, in essence, from the men who built the British Empire, men "who had entered the old progression, learned the old rules, played the old games" (IA, p. 259).

Feminist analysis discovers that Anthony Keating's "religion", whether expressed in sacral or secular terms, is a patriarchal philosophy of power, derived from a dualistic metaphysics. Mind and matter are first seen as separate; then it is asserted that mind is superior to and must govern matter. While this philosophy has at times consoled the oppressed, it is ultimately the cause of their oppression. When it ceases to be merely a private consolation and becomes the basis for public policy, it can and perhaps inevitably will lead to urban redevelopment schemes where buildings count for more than people, to wars fought for ideals and principles, to final solutions and Armageddon.

The old games and the new, the progressions and processions of men, have been mercilessly exposed for the deadly war games and funeral processions they are, by Virginia Woolf in *Three Guineas* and by Mary Daly in *Gyn/Ecology*. But although Margaret Drabble ends this novel with a bleak view of one woman's situation in a man-made world, I am not at all sure that she would make Woolf's and Daly's association between male philosophies and phallocratic necrophilia. Not only does she render in this novel the poetic power of the vision which has shaped patriarchal culture but here, as in *The Needle's Eye*, she exempts patriarchal religion from feminist scrutiny. However severely she, as well as Alison Murry, may indict men for the games they play, from poker to property deals, she will not see that the biggest game of all is what John Fowles, in *The Magus*, calls "the God Game". "Into some of Anthony's experience", she believes, "we [i.e., women] can enter. We can appreciate, for instance, his interest in birds" (IA, p. 295).

The Ice Age opens with a bird, a pheasant who falls dead of a heart attack onto Anthony Keating's pond. Anthony identifies with the pheasant because he too has had a heart attack. Moreover he thinks of his heart as "a bird, a delicate creature that must not be shocked or offended" (IA, p. 6). The sight of the gasometer "lifted [Anthony's] heart. Up soared the heart like a bird in the chest" (IA, p. 28). Citing *The Garrick Year* and *The Needle's Eye*, Nancy Hardin remarked to Drabble that she frequently presented the spirit as a bird, and Drabble agreed: "The spirit of a person is like a bird trapped in his body. The cage is the body – definitely a Platonic notion". Definitely dualistic.

In prison, Anthony "takes pleasure in observing" birds who, unlike him, "are free, they fly in and out freely". Watching the birds, "his heart rises, he experiences hope" (IA, p. 295). "I have this deep conviction", Drabble told Barbara Milton, "that if you were to get high up enough over the world, you would see things that look like coincidence are, in fact, part of a pattern. This sounds very mystical and ridiculous, but I don't think it is. . . . I suppose it is perfectly possible that one will die without knowing what [the pattern] was all about. But I have this deep faith that it will all be revealed to me one day. One day I shall just see into the heart of the whole thing. . . . Maybe when I'm ten years older I'll decide that I was just deluding myself. But I haven't yet got to that stage". At this stage, Margaret Drabble – like Bunyan, like Rose Vassiliou, like Anthony Keating – is apparently "prepared to bet on the existence of God".

What her last three novels suggest is that Margaret Drabble's chief difficulty is not writing about men. On the contrary. What she seems to find difficult, if not impossible, is giving her whole-hearted support to female characters who are radically feminist in their critique of patriarchy. Kitty Friedmann adopts Anthony Keating's strategy for dealing with the terrible times we live in: she refuses "to contemplate the possibility of evil" (IA, p. 59). She is presented as a good woman, almost a saint. Maureen Kirby, Drabble thinks, is "the nicest of this perhaps unrepresentative group of British citizens" who populate *The Ice Age* (IA, p. 189). Maureen is rewarded by a happy ending. She marries Derek Ashby, who persuades her that she ought to become a business executive herself. Because "Maureen [is] a sophisticated creature, in her own way, good at playing games" (IA, p. 226), she makes it to the top. Drabble calls her "a lucky woman" (IA, p. 244).

More gracefully and contentedly than Rose Vassiliou, but no less absolutely, Kitty Friedmann and Maureen Kirby accept and accede to the male point of view. The only female in Drabble's last three novels who doesn't, Frances Wingate, is presented in such a way by her author that we cannot quite take her seriously. Obstreperous women, who give signs of wanting to sabotage the whole male endeavour, are muted like Emily Offenbach or undeveloped like Alison Murray. "Her life is beyond imagining. It will not be imagined." At least not yet, by Margaret Drabble.

Why not? Well, for one thing, although she has no objection to calling herself a woman writer (she considers the sexual adjective "descriptive," not "discriminative"),[9] Drabble has indicated at various points in her writing career that she resents any suggestion that she should limit herself to women's subject matter or women's point of view.[10] It is an issue that concerns many women writers, this question of whether or not there is a body of experience and sensibility to which women are confined because of their sex. "Does a 'woman writer' have a separate psychology – by virtue of being a woman?" Cynthia Ozick asked in a recent issue of *Ms.* magazine.[11] "Does a 'woman writer' have a separate body of ideas – by virtue of being a woman? Does a 'woman writer' have a body of separate experience – by virtue of being a woman?" Angrily, she rejects what she calls "the literary credo of the new feminism", which proposes that women write about female experience. "When I write", she declares, "I am free. I am, as a writer, whatever I wish to become. I can think myself into a male, or a female, or a stone, or a raindrop, or a block of wood, or a Tibetan, or the leg of a mosquito". Addressing the same issue, Janet Burroway added that "to suppose that what a writer 'knows' is bounded by her or his specific experience is to misunderstand not only the author's capacity but the reader's. Literature works because people can feel what they have not experienced".

This is an appealing and persuasive argument. But one must be careful, as I am not convinced Ozick is, to distinguish between the subject matter which is legitimately available to the woman writer and her point of view. It is one thing to write about men and their world and quite another to write like a man.

A woman writer *does* (or should) have a separate psychology, a separate body of ideas and experiences "by virtue of being a woman". That psychology, those ideas and experiences, make up what Burroway calls the "feminist" point of view. "Women have no doubt been attracted to literature as a profession", she writes, "because it is antiauthoritarian; it rejects the knowledge of fact, category, and definition". Even Ozick judges the proponents of "women's writing" against the standards of what she calls "classical feminism", which "was conceived of as the end of false barriers and boundaries; as the end of segregationist fictions and lies".

It has frequently been urged by many men and some women that this attitude be labelled "humanist" rather than "feminist," and certainly I would agree that the goal of feminism is the recognition that all persons, of both sexes, are complex individuals, irreducible to either stereotype or type. But it is important to preserve the distinction between "feminism" and "humanism," because historically, what we call humanism – whether classical or Christian – is dyed through and through with patriarchal dualism. From Plato to Descartes, humanists have distinguished between soul and body, *res cogitans* and *res extensa* and – let us not blink the fact – male and female. Existentialism is a humanistic philosophy, and we have seen that when the feminist Simone de Beauvoir thinks like an existentialist, she thinks like a man.

Margaret Drabble's last three novels, *The Needle's Eye*, *The Realms of Gold*, and *The Ice Age*, demonstrate quite effectively that like George Eliot, the woman writer she most admires, she can imaginatively appropriate and convincingly portray male experience. These novels also reveal that Drabble has done more than imagine what men must feel and believe and value; she has to some extent endorsed it. Ironically, the woman who perceived the basic contradiction between de Beauvoir's feminism and her humanism has herself moved from the feminist vision of *The Waterfall* to something which must be called humanism in *The Ice Age*, whose epigraph invokes the spirit of John Milton, one of history's most notorious misogynists.

It may be that the extremity of her vision frightened Drabble. As she has said, "you have to be careful what you imagine, because the act of imagining is the act of encouraging yourself to be a certain kind of person".[12] The final section of *The Second Sex* is called

"Toward Liberation". In it, de Beauvoir writes that "it is through gainful employment that woman has traversed most of the distance that separated her from the male; and nothing else can guarantee her liberty in practice" (TSS, p. 639). "The independent woman" is economically independent of men. The kind of woman Drabble imagines in Jane Gray, Emily Offenbach, and Frances Wingate is independent in ways Simone de Beauvoir, writing in 1949, had not yet conceived. Creating these characters, Drabble glimpses the possibility that we women may free ourselves from men's domination not only of our bodies and our labour, but of our thoughts. Intuitively perhaps, she understands that feminism is not primarily a set of issues or policies but a radical and transformative way of perceiving reality. By exorcising the internalized metaphysics and ontology of patriarchy which have victimized us in the past, women may claim the right to live fully and authentically. This is a heady prospect, and a sobering one. For it means that we must reject the philosophies and modes of perception which have formed and nurtured us.

Patriarchy has taught us that we are the other and has given us ways of being the other. If we deny that we are the other, then who are we? If we refuse the identities patriarchy has given us, what are we left with? "Becoming who we are", Mary Daly writes, "requires existential   courage   to   confront   the   experience   of nothingness . . . [and] at this point in history women are in a unique sense called to be the bearers of existential courage in society".[13] It is an awesome burden. Few women are willing to assume it and even fewer to acknowledge that this is what feminism demands.

When asked to account for her popularity, Margaret Drabble usually replies that it's probably because she's an "ordinary" person. "There are an awful lot of people like me", she told one interviewer[14] and added, to another, "a lot of people have got exactly the same worries and problems".[15] What neither Drabble nor those interviewers commented on is the interesting fact that her novels are particularly popular with women readers. In view of that fact, her remarks about her "ordinariness" assume significance. To me, Drabble seems not so much ordinary as exemplary. For the women who constitute the bulk of her readership, her novels embody their own deep-seated ambivalence about feminism, with its exhilarating vision and its terrifying challenge.

Margaret Drabble's novels remind me of certain drawings

psychologists use to illustrate what they call figural ambiguity. Perhaps the most famous of these "equivocal figures"[16] is the wife/mother-in-law picture. Some viewers perceive it as the profile of a beautiful young woman, with a graceful, sinuous neck. Others see that delicate profile as the warty nose of an aged crone, and the swan-like neck as her toothless, sunken jaw. Psychologists tell us that which image we perceive depends to a great extent on our expectations, which are derived from our experience.

What interests me about these drawings and makes me think of them in connection with Drabble's novels is that both images are latently present in the drawing. Whichever one consciously perceives, the other is at least subliminally available. Depending on a woman's expectations and experience, she can read Drabble's novels, especially the recent ones, as radical feminist visions or as affirmations of traditional humanist values. But whichever message she consciously reads in these novels, she will be subliminally absorbing the other contradictory one. And this, I think, accounts for Drabble's popularity with women readers, since most women are as ambivalent about feminism as Margaret Drabble is. Her novels offer them a chance to have their cake and eat it.

I have no way of verifying this hypothesis except to appeal to my own experience. I read Margaret Drabble for the first time in 1972, when *The Needle's Eye* was enthusiastically reviewed by Joyce Carol Oates on the front page of the *New York Times Book Review*. I was so impressed with that novel that I rounded up and read all the earlier ones. When I finished reading, I wanted to articulate my response to Drabble's fiction and so wrote what turned out to be my first published essay, which appeared in an issue of *Critique* devoted to women writers.[17]

In that essay, I quote Emma Evans as she muses on the death of Julian: "I used to be like Julian myself, but now I have two children, and you will not find me at the bottom of any river. I have grown into the earth. I am terrestrial". "What grounds Emma", I wrote, "is her womanhood, that resilient strength which 'time and maternity' have wrought. Similarly", I went on, "Rosamund discovers her womanhood at the end of *The Millstone*, which is both her achievement and the measure of her superiority over the father of her illegitimate child". I ended the essay praising Rose Vassiliou for "accept[ing] the necessary limitations of [her] humanity" in renouncing for Christopher what I clearly regarded as a specious "grace".

In 1972 I was an anorexic housewife, bored with domesticity and small children, increasingly alienated from and hostile towards my husband, frightened to admit the situation and guilty about it. What I saw in Drabble's novels was what this personal situation prepared me to see: self-denial, renunciation, an equation of womanhood with gritting one's teeth and bearing it.

I have no way of knowing whether or to what extent I was also unconsciously responding to the Beauvoirian call for liberation in those novels. I do know that by 1974 I had a divorce, a Ph.D., a job at Dartmouth, the respect of my children, and the beginnings of a sense of self-esteem. Since then, with the support and encouragement of the feminist community here at Dartmouth, I have come more and more to value my worth as a scholar and as a person who is also a woman. Now when I read Drabble I see what this book has just described. But while I now respond primarily to the visionary message of her novels, I know – from my own history more than from objective, critical analysis – that the conservative message is still there, still being voiced, however inaudible it may be to women who hear, in *The Realms of Gold* for instance, a ringing affirmation of female autonomy.

"Do you ever find critics useful?" Barbara Milton asked Margaret Drabble. "Sometimes", she answered. "I find what they call 'constructive' criticism helpful. Occasionally you come across somebody who says, 'Why didn't she do so and so?' And you think, 'God, why didn't I?' And he [sic] says, 'Why doesn't she do so and so next time?' And you think, 'Yes, why don't I?' " It is in the spirit of constructive criticism that I have written this book, not to ask "Why didn't Drabble do so and so?" but to acknowledge and applaud her feminist vision and encourage her to give it freer rein in the future. I would like her to recognize that having one's cake and eating it is a barmecide feast. To borrow her own words, I want her next novel to be "not only a book but a future", an unequivocally feminist blueprint.

NOTES

1 Milton, op. cit.
2 Ibid.
3 Gussow, op. cit.
4 Margaret Drabble, *The Ice Age* (New York: Alfred A. Knopf, 1977), p. 33. Further references to IA will appear in the text.
5 Cf. Frances Wingate's paradisal ditch in *The Realms of Gold*, with its newts and celandines, "a whole unnecessary and teeming world of creation" (RG, p. 103).
6 Gussow, op. cit.
7 Milton, op. cit.
8 Boethius, *The Consolation of Philosophy*, trans. Richard Green (New York: Bobbs-Merrill, 1962). I am quoting in this paragraph from the translator's introduction.
9 "A Woman Writer", op. cit.
10 See especially her statements to Nancy Poland and Mel Gussow, op. cit.
11 "Does Genius Have a Gender?" *Ms.* (December 1977), pp. 56–57, 79–81, 83–84.
12 Milton, op. cit.
13 *Beyond God the Father*, p. 23.
14 Clare, op. cit.
15 Poland, op. cit.
16 My thanks to Beverly Shedd and Peter Robbie of Dartmouth's Visual Studies program, who helped me discover the name of these drawings and thus the title of my book.
17 Ellen Cronan Rose, "Margaret Drabble: Surviving the Future", *Critique*, Vol. 15, No. 1 (1973), 5–21.

List of Works Cited

I   BOOKS BY MARGARET DRABBLE

Arnold Bennett. New York: Alfred A. Knopf, 1974.
The Garrick Year. 1964; rpt. New York: Morrow, 1965.
The Ice Age. New York: Alfred A. Knopf, 1977.
Jerusalem the Golden. 1967; rpt. New York: Popular Library, 1977.
The Millstone. 1965; rpt. as *Thank You All Very Much*, New York; New American Library, 1969.
The Needle's Eye. New York: Alfred A. Knopf, 1972.
The Realms of Gold. New York: Alfred A. Knopf, 1975.
A Summer Bird-Cage. 1962; rpt. New York: Belmont Books, 1971.
The Waterfall. New York: Alfred A. Knopf, 1969.

II   STORIES, ARTICLES, AND REVIEWS BY MARGARET DRABBLE

"The Author Comments" on Monica Lauritzen Mannheimer, "The Search for Identity in Margaret Drabble's *The Needle's Eye*". *Dutch Quarterly Review of Anglo-American Letters*, Vol. 5, No. 1 (1975), 35–38.
"Cassandra in a World Under Seige". *Ramparts*, Vol. 10, No. 8 (February 1972), 50–54.
"The Fearful Fame of Arnold Bennett", *Observer* (May 11, 1967), pp. 12–14.
"Hassan's Tower", in *Winter's Tales 12*, ed. A. D. Maclean. London: Macmillan, 1966.
"Revelations and Prophecies". *Saturday Review* (May 27, 1978), pp. 54, 56.
"Say a Good Word for the Curse". *Good Housekeeping* (English edition), February 1978, p. 51.
"A Woman Writer", *Books*, No. 11 (Spring 1973), 4–6.

III   INTERVIEWS WITH MARGARET DRABBLE

Coleman, Terry. "A Biographer Waylaid by Novels". *Guardian*, 106 (April 15, 1972), 23.

Firchow, Peter, ed. "Margaret Drabble". *The Writer's Place: Interviews on the Literary Situation in Contemporary Britain.* Minneapolis: University of Minnesota Press, 1974, pp. 102–121.

Gussow, Mel. "Margaret Drabble: A Double Life". *The New York Times Book Review* (October 9, 1977), pp. 40–41.

Hardin, Nancy S. "An Interview with Margaret Drabble". *Contemporary Literature*, Vol. 14, No. 3 (Summer 1973), 273–295.

Milton, Barbara. "Margaret Drabble: The Art of Fiction LXX". *The Paris Review*, No. 74 (Fall-Winter 1978), 40–65.

Poland, Nancy. "Margaret Drabble: 'There Must Be a Lot of People Like Me' ". *Midwest Quarterly*, Vol. XVI, No. 3 (Spring 1975), 255–267.

Preussner, Dee. "Interview with Margaret Drabble". Forthcoming in *Modern Fiction Studies*.

IV   OTHER WORKS CITED

Alter, Robert. *Rogue's Progress: Studies in the Picaresque Novel.* Cambridge: Harvard University Press, 1964.

Barstow, Anne. "The Uses of Archaeology for Women's History: James Mellaart's Work on the Neolithic Goddess at Catal Huyuk". *Feminist Studies*, Vol. 4, No. 3 (October 1978).

Beards, Virginia K. "Margaret Drabble: Novels of a Cautious Feminist". *Critique*, Vol. 15, No. 1 (1973), 35–47.

Beauvoir, Simone de. *The Second Sex*, trans. H. M. Parshley. New York: Alfred A. Knopf, 1953.

Bennett, Arnold. *Clayhanger*. 1910; rpt. New York: Doubleday, Doran & Company, Inc., 1936.

——. *Hilda Lessways*. 1911; rpt. New York: Doubleday, Doran & Company, Inc., 1936.

——. *A Man From the North*. 1898; rpt. New York: George H. Doran Company, 1911.

Bergonzi, Bernard. *The Situation of the Novel*. London: Macmillan, 1970.

Boethius. *The Consolation of Philosophy*, trans. Richard Green. New York: Bobbs–Merrill, 1962.

Bruch, Hilde. *Eating Disorders: Obesity, Anorexia Nervosa, and the Person Within*. New York: Basic Books, 1973.

Buckley, Jerome Hamilton. *Season of Youth: The Bildungsroman from Dickens to Golding*. Cambridge: Harvard University Press, 1974.

Burroway, Janet and Cynthia Ozick. "Does Genius Have a Gender?" *Ms.* (December 1977), pp. 56–57, 79–81, 83–84.

Byatt, A. S. *The Game*. New York: Scribner's, 1967.

Chesler, Phyllis. *Women and Madness*. New York: Doubleday, 1972.

Chodorow, Nancy. *The Reproduction of Mothering: Psychoanalysis and the Sociology of Gender*. Berkeley: University of California Press, 1978.

Christ, Carol P. and Judith Plaskow, eds. *Womanspirit Rising: A Feminist Reader in Religion*. New York: Harper Forum Books, 1979.

Clare, John. "Margaret Drabble's Everyday Hell". (London) *Times* (March 27, 1972), p. 6.

Daly, Mary. *Beyond God the Father: Toward a Philosophy of Women's Liberation*. Boston: Beacon Press, 1973.

——. *Gyn/Ecology: the Metaethics of Radical Feminism*. Boston: Beacon Press, 1978.

deFord, Sara and Clarinda Harriss Lott. *Forms of Verse*. New York: Appleton–Century–Crofts, 1971.

Denne, Constance Ayers and Katharine M. Rogers. "Women Novelists: A Distinct Group?" *Women's Studies*, Vol. 3, No. 1 (1975), 5–28.

Didion, "The Women's Movement".*The New York Times Book Review* (July 30, 1972), p. 14.

Dinnerstein, Dorothy. *The Mermaid and the Minotaur: Sexual Arrangements and Human Malaise*. New York: Harper & Row, 1976.

Edel, Leon. *Literary Biography*. 1959; rpt. Bloomington: Indiana University Press, 1973.

Ellmann, Mary. *Thinking About Women*. New York: Harcourt, Brace, 1968.

Friedl, Ernestine. *Women and Men: An Anthropologist's View*. New York: Holt, Rinehart, and Winston, 1975.

Goldenberg, Naomi R. *Changing of the Gods: Feminism and the End of Traditional Religions*. Boston: Beacon Press, 1979.

Griffin, Susan. *Woman and Nature: the Roaring inside Her*. New York: Harper & Row, 1978.

Hardin, Nancy S. "Drabble's *The Millstone*: A Fable for Our Times". *Critique*, Vol. 15, No. 1 (1973), 22–34.

Leighton, Jean. *Simone de Beauvoir on Woman*. Rutherford, N. J.: Fairleigh Dickinson University Press, 1975.

Lessing, Doris. *Briefing for a Descent into Hell*. New York: Alfred A. Knopf, 1971.

Libby, Marion Vlastos. "Fate and Feminism in the Novels of Margaret Drabble". *Contemporary Literature*, Vol. 16, No. 2 (Spring 1975), 175–192.

MacCarthy, Fiona. "The Drabble Sisters". *Guardian* (April 13, 1975), p. 8.

Milton, John. *Complete Poems and Major Prose*, ed. Merritt Y. Hughes. Indianapolis: The Odyssey Press, 1957.

Moers, Ellen. *Literary Women: The Great Writers*. New York: Anchor Books, 1977.

Morgan, Robin. *Going Too Far: The Personal Chronicle of a Feminist*. New York: Random House, 1977.

Myer, Valerie Grosvenor. *Margaret Drabble: Puritanism and Permissiveness*. New York: Barnes and Noble, 1974.

Palazzoli, Mara Selvini. *Self-Starvation* (1963), trans. Arnold Pomerans. London: Human Context Books, 1974.

Reiter, Rayna R., ed. *Toward an Anthropology of Women*. New York and London: Monthly Review Press, 1975.

Rich, Adrienne. *Of Woman Born: Motherhood as Experience and Institution*. New York: Bantam Books, 1977.

Rosaldo, Michelle Zimbalist and Louise Lamphere, eds. *Woman, Culture, and Society*. Stanford: Stanford University Press, 1974.

Rose, Ellen Cronan. "Margaret Drabble: Surviving the Future". *Critique*, Vol. 15, No. 1 (1973), 5–21.

Ruether, Rosemary Radford. *New Woman/New Earth: Sexist Ideologies and Human Liberation*. New York: Seabury Press, 1975.

Sale, Roger. "Huxley and Bennett, Bedford and Drabble". *Hudson Review*, Vol. XXVIII, No. 2 (Summer 1975), 289.

——. "The Realms of Gold". *Hudson Review*, Vol. 28, No. 4 (Winter 1975–76), 628.

Seneca. *Oedipus*, trans. Moses Hadas. New York: The Liberal Arts Press, 1955.

Showalter, Elaine. *A Literature of Their Own*. Princeton: Princeton University Press, 1977.

Spacks, Patricia Meyer. *The Female Imagination*. New York: Alfred A. Knopf, 1975.

Wolff, Cynthia Griffin. *A Feast of Words: The Triumph of Edith Wharton*. New York: Oxford University Press, 1977.

Zeman, Anthea. *Presumptuous Girls: Women and Their World in the Serious Woman's Novel*. London: George Weidenfeld & Nicolson, 1977.

Index

Abbreviations of titles of novels used in index entries for characters are: GY = *The Garrick Year*; IA = *The Ice Age*; JG = *Jerusalem the Golden*; M = *The Millstone*; NE = *The Needle's Eye*; RG = *The Realms of Gold*; SBC = *A Summer Bird-Cage*; W = *The Waterfall*.